# STRONG INSIDE
## A RELENTLESS PURSUIT OF CONTINUOUS IMPROVEMENT

JOHN D'ALESSANDRO

ISBN: 0692269169
ISBN 13: 9780692269169

I am so very grateful for the kindness of others. I am so appreciative of so many who have endured such terrible circumstances before me. Thank you for pushing forward and continuing to exist. Thank you to the innocent children who prove to me each day that love truly does still reside, and can inspire, in the darkest of places. Thank you to all the people of service who continue with selfless acts that help so many in need. I thank you for your example. I am grateful for any and every piece of art or music that has relayed stories of struggle and encouragement, I thank you for your voice. I am appreciative of the many stories in forms of entertainment that relieve my stress and inspire me to do more. I thank those friends and family that have pure hearts and are always there if needed.

I am grateful for all my adversities and people who oppose my progress. I am grateful to those with such anger, hate, and jealously, and how your resistance strengthens me. I am grateful for the bad examples that help me understand why I should choose to do good actions. I am grateful every day for a chance to experience and learn from both my mistakes and accomplishments. I am grateful for the chance to evolve and build, not only for myself, but for the next generation. I see value in all things and accept the challenge of overcoming wrong in order to appreciate right. I appreciate the journey and opportunities that lie ahead.


-John D'Alessandro

# CONTENTS-

*What's Stopping You?*

*Heroes and Work Ethic*

*Talent and Effort*

*Do It*

*Dreams*

*Play Your Role*

*Change*

## **RECOGNIZE-OVERCOME-EVOLVE**

*Adversity*

*Fear*

*Doubt*

*Emotions*

*Gossip*

*Judging*

*Temptation*

*Laziness*

*Consequence*

*Man in the mirror*

*Mr. Perfect Became A Victim of Pride*

## BUILDING CHARACTER & CONTINUOUS IMPROVEMENT

*Character*

*Building Good Characteristics*

*Coward*

*Leadership*

*Responsibility*

*Accountability*

*Discipline*

*Honesty*

*Patience*

*Sacrifice*

*Service*

*I AM LEGEND*


## THE BASICS

*Education*

*Read*

*Humility in Learning*

*Simplicity*

*Communication*

*Time*

## FOREWORD

H. PJ Peterson Youth America International

My wife, Melodie, and I have been in the youth rehabilitation and counseling business for well over Twenty years. We have a 501-(c)-(3) organization built for the same purpose. Throughout our years of helping young people to see their world from a different, but positive prospective, we realized early on in their development that they were all seeking the same things in life that we all do. We also concluded that they needed support, love, understanding, and a sense of belonging. Many young people today have a pretty good idea of where they want to be, but have no concept of how to get there. Many times when they do attempt to find their way to their goals, they get lost and find themselves in trouble more times than not. They are naive and some lack understanding and knowledge. They are quick to blame society and others for their failures. For the most part, they are good people and are fun to be with. They are intelligent and some have developed incredible street smarts to survive. I often wonder if I could make it, if given the same predicament.

After reading *Strong Inside*, I realized that John has captured the essence of the struggles most of these young people are plagued with. I am certain that his take on the problems facing these youths can be related to by his troubled peers. One of the critical facts that we found out from talking with these troubled youths, is that the first people they turn to for help is each other. They seem to automatically form a support group of like-minded people to find support from. They will turn to each other for help before they turn to their parents or other adults. John has gone through most if not all that these young people are struggling with. The most important part of John's excerpts that I find most intriguing is the fact that he offers his own experiences of dealing with his struggles without passing judgment. In my opinion he understands and sympathizes with these young people better than many so called experts or authority figures. Again, since he too has witnessed and experienced many of the trials and tribulations that many of today's troubled young men and women may be going through, I believe they will be naturally drawn to his words of perseverance and improvement.

1

I am not saying that John's book is the fix-all remedy to what's troubling our future generation. It is, however, a wonderful alternative for finding their way out of the many difficulties they may be facing. I highly recommend John's book, "Strong Inside – A Relentless Pursuit of Continuous Improvement" whether you are a parent looking for insight into what your' child may be thinking or going through, or if you are a young person searching for understanding and guidance from someone similar to you and even if you are just looking for encouraging and inspiring words, this book is for you.
All the best

# ABOUT THE AUTHOR

My name is John D'Alessandro. I am an Italian, Samoan, American. I was born to teenage parents in Honolulu, Hawaii November 19, 1977. Though I dreaded it at the time I was blessed with the opportunity to move frequently, often state to state and even to another country throughout my adolescent years. My parent's divorced when I was seven years old. My mother re-married when I was eleven. Both of my fathers were military men. I also spent my high school years with my grandparents. My uncles on my mother's side also provided some male influence during my childhood years.

I come from an exceptionally large family. During my younger years I have lived with family that, were very privileged to say the least. I also lived with family that, come from the humblest of beginnings. I stayed with family and friends that stressed religion and the importance of faith in our Heavenly Father. I've been with family and friends that had no real spiritual belief what so ever. I am related to or know those with degrees from wonderful educational establishments. I also have relationships with those that have gained education from the streets and some who are considered exceptional in a whole other element; however they are considered very educated none-the-less. I actually know a few professionals on both sides of the spectrum that are, or at one time were great at what they do. Most of my family and friends are middle class "average everyday citizens" trying to make an honest living and provide a better future with more opportunities for those dear to them.

I share this with you without giving too much information in order to protect the privacy of those in my life. I am not going too name drop or give to many egocentric stories to gain credibility or create some form of nostalgia. What I would like to do is give you a better understanding of who I am and how I've been lucky to gain much perspective in my life through experience. I've been intrigued by the power of the streets hustle. I have felt the rush of competing athletically. I know the struggle of hard labor with little or no reward. I have experienced the power of corporate America and the greed of money and the ego involved with managing others. I know the downfall of anger, stubbornness and family quarrels. I know how it feels to be ashamed and to let down those dear to you. I've seen the power of change and selflessness.

I know the hunger for knowledge, meaning, and purpose. I know the kindness of service and giving. I have faith in an above power and I believe in the good of myself and others. I understand that as much as I think I know, in reality I know very little and must continue to improve.

Tupac Shakur once said, "I might not change the world but my words may help spark the mind that will." Those words give me such inspiration. I want to learn from every experience whether it be a death of a friend or a birth of my child. I want to gain understanding from those dear to me and those misunderstood. I want to make a choice to live, grow, and evolve into what I hope becomes a better human being. Throughout this process, I want to share and give perspective to others. I want to give understanding to gain understanding. If I have felt remorse and sorrow, then maybe I can relate to your pain. If I know addiction, then maybe I might be able to share your struggle. If I can appreciate happiness and sacrifice then hopefully I have a better understanding of what love is. I hope to share thoughts that help provoke thoughts. I want to share my experiences and show how a lack of knowledge, understanding, and the inability to adapt or change could really blind us with ignorance. Ultimately, it is ignorance that will block us from reaching our potential and from evolving into the persons we can become and probably truly want to be. I want us to help each other by building a strong moral foundation, and a loving, humbling, strength, from within. I want us to inspire each other on our relentless pursuit of continuous improvement.

## ABOUT THE BOOK

**"With understanding we can strengthen relationships, revitalize neighborhoods, unify nations, and even bring peace to a troubled world. Without it chaos, intolerance, hate, and war are often the result."- M. Russell Ballard**

You know that feeling you get when the world is crumbling around you. You are absolutely mad enough to yell and scream and also sad enough to tear. Do you remember the words or actions that lifted you up out of that dark hole? Even if only temporarily we have all had moments of hope, inspiration, and perseverance. Many of these moments have emerged while facing numerous obstacles placed in our paths of continued improvement. Ask yourself, "Are you strong inside?"

Many of us are lost in false ideas and easy outcomes. We live in a world of convenience and mediocrity. There are too many of us that are looking for excuses rather than for answers. To many times in our lives we fail to recognize the errors in our ways yet we are quick to judge and blame others. Through our behavior and development it becomes very difficult for us to criticize ourselves. We become so arrogant that we ignore signs and close doors that may help us evolve into stronger and better people. Ask yourself again "Am I truly strong inside?" Are you strong enough to accept when you are wrong? Can you learn from your mistakes and recognize the person that you truly want to be? Do you have the strength to take on the burden of the responsibility of your choices, overcome failure, and remain committed to your goals? Are you willing to grow, become a better person, and share your kindness with others?

To become stronger, I had to weaken my ego and pride. I had to realize and accept that I was not in the place where I wanted to be in my life. Placing my failures on others, procrastinating, and losing direction was getting me nowhere. I wanted so much more and realized that in order to achieve great things I had to work so much harder. I reminded myself that every day is an opportunity and chance to grow and every day that passes is a part of my life that is gone forever. I have to make sure that I take the challenge of fulfilling each day and opportunity with great effort and understanding. It is never too late for us to start becoming what we were always meant to be. I want to accept the challenge of living and achieving. I have a burning desire to share my journey and thoughts with others.

I am writing this book because it is a goal of mine to do something good and fulfilling with the opportunities I have. I want to accomplish something of meaning that will be left here on this earth throughout time. I want to write a book that my family and friends will be proud of, offer words that will uplift and inspire. I want this book to be somewhat of a handbook for those in need of a friendly word and a bit of understanding. I want to share my thoughts, feelings, and ideas. I want people to read these pages and say "Yes, I've definitely felt like that before." Or maybe they may have never felt that way before or experienced a certain situation. Hopefully, these words can bring a different perspective to some and a better understanding to others on certain subjects and feelings. I want to provoke thought. I want people to know that they always have a choice. I want them to know that it is never too late to learn, never too late to grow, never too late to change and that they most definitely never have to give up. Life is not always fair but opportunity is all around us. I want to share things that may help with life and it's many obstacles and struggles, especially for any individual that may have no one to turn to. I want to write this book because it is something that I truly believe in. Many times in our lives we do not accomplish our wants and dreams. We fall victim to excuses and circumstances. In many cases we never put forth the effort and determination needed in order to make these goals and desires a reality. I want others to realize that inspiration, meaning, and purpose lies within us all. I want others to understand their delicate spirit and help improve their inner strength. I hope this book can be a friendly push or reminder that when we believe, sacrifice and work hard enough, anything is possible, no matter what the odds. We can do anything we set our minds to if we believe in ourselves. Together we can hope, endure, and believe through all things!

"If you want to awaken all of humanity,

then awaken all of yourself. Truly the greatest

gift you have to give is that

of your own self-transformation."

-Lao Tzu

Did you push yourself to be great today?

If not you lost a day.

How many days do you have to lose?

Push yourself to find the greatness inside you.

It is always easy to be average.

Do everything you can to be your best today.

Every day after this one push yourself to be even better.

Never ever give up!

# A BETTER ME

There is no passion
to be found
in settling for a life
that is less than
the one you are
capable of living

-Nelson Mandela-

# RECOGNIZE WHO WE ARE AND WHAT MATTERS TO US
## WHAT IS THE BLUEPRINT TO OUR SUCCESS?

**"If everybody was satisfied with himself, There
would be no heroes."
-Mark Twain**

Are you frustrated going through the motions of life? Are you bored with no plans or motivation? Well if you are feeling down and lost it is probably a good thing. It means that you are not comfortable with settling and carry a natural desire to improve. Recognition is the first step in acknowledging our life's purpose and plan. We can't change if we don't recognize what we need to improve upon.

Acknowledge your failures. Do not run away from your mishaps. Do not rationalize your failed attempts and the reasons why you failed. We all fail at times. The real question is, are we content with failing? Remember we always have a choice. No matter how far we've gone down a wrong road, we always have the choice to turn back or get off that path. Like in chess, sometimes you have to move backward in order to move ahead.

Ask yourself, "What matters to me?" Whatever you believe in deserves attention. It has been said, "If you do not stand for some meaning or purpose you could fall for anything." What are the things that are important to you? Why do they have such meaning? Are you willing to give your heart and soul to these beliefs? Discover what it is you truly want and give yourself to it.

Preparation is the key to success. Prepare for your future with the understanding of your past. Being unprepared is how we welcome failure and provoke it to succeed. Be the most prepared and dedicated to your vision. Prepare for opportunities to present themselves and be ready to seize the moment.

Our success will come through our actions, not what we intend to do. Our greatest step is the first step. Without a beginning there can be no end. So much time is wasted making excuses or building confidence or comfort to begin our journey. Take action and do it. You can do anything. Sometimes we just need a little help figuring it out. Our dreams are our visions and concepts. We must take action to understand these experiences. Be bold. Make bold choices and live your wonderful life. Create your masterpiece. Your story has not yet been written.

"A man should conceive of a legitimate purpose in his heart, and set out to accomplish it. He should make this purpose the centralizing point of his thoughts. It may take the form of a spiritual ideal, or it may be a worldly object, according to his nature at the time being; but whichever it is, he should steadily focus his thought forces upon the object which he has set before him. He should make this purpose his supreme duty, and should devote himself to its attainment, not allowing his thoughts to wander away into ephemeral fancies, longings, and imaginings. This is the royal road to self-control and true concentration of thought. Even if he fails again and again to accomplish his purpose (as he necessarily must until weakness is overcome), the strength of character gained will be the measure of his true success, and this will form a new starting point for future power and triumph."
**-James Allen**

## "A Parent Talks to a Child Before the First Game"

## by former UCLA Coach John Wooden

This is your first game, my child. I hope you win. I hope you win for your sake, not mine. Because winning's nice. It's a good feeling. Like the whole world is yours. But, it passes, this feeling. And what lasts is what you've learned. And what you learn about is life. That's what sports is all about. Life. The whole thing is played out in an afternoon. The happiness of life. The miseries. The joys. The heartbreaks.

There's no telling what'll turn up. There's no telling whether they'll toss you out in the first five minutes or whether you'll stay for the long haul. There's no telling how you'll do. You might be a hero or you might be absolutely nothing. There's just no telling. Too much depends on chance. On how the ball bounces.

I'm not talking about the game, my child. I'm talking about life. But it's life that the game is all about. Just as I said. Because every game is life. And life is a game. A serious game. Dead serious. But that's what you do with serious things. You do your best. You take what comes. And you run with it. Winning is fun. Sure. But winning is not the point. Wanting to win is the point. Not giving up is the point. Never being satisfied with what you've done is the point. Never letting up is the point. Never letting anyone down is the point. Play to win. Sure. But lose like a champion. Because it's not winning that counts. What counts is tryin

## DO YOU

"Every choice moves us closer to or farther away from
something. Where are your choices taking your life? What do
your behaviors demonstrate that you are saying yes or no to in
life?"
**-Eric Allenbaugh**


Create your own way. Think of all the attributes that you may
appreciate in others. Take time to ponder what characteristics you
admire in those people you look up to. Understand that you posses'
the ability to develop those same qualities. Recognize that you have
the ability to be whatever it is you decide to be. Our most
accomplished moments will occur when we are given the opportunity
to make choices of character. We were given life. It is our choice how
we will live that life. We will not be judged by how we were raised,
how we were loved, or what our intentions are. We will be judged on
our actions, our influence on others and how we choose to love. Be
real with yourself and recognize the power of your choices. Create
your own experience. There is no better opportunity in life than the
opportunity to live one. Your possibilities are endless. Have the
confidence in yourself to pursue your dreams. When it is all said and
done you alone will know if you are at peace with the way you guided
yourself through life's journey. Hopefully you are able to touch others
enough that they appreciate being able to participate in your journey
as well. Wherever you are at this time in your life is a perfect place to
start being who you want to be. It is never too late to be what you
might have been. Dare to be everything you can be. You can do it.
Ultimately, the choice is yours.


"Man is made or unmade by himself. By the right choice he
ascends. As a being of power, intelligence, and love, and the
lord of his own thoughts, he holds the key to every situation."
**-James Allen**

## MOTIVATION

Who and what motivates us? Every day there are instances, samples and illustrations of great inspiration consuming the world we live in. A favorite song, an exciting speech, a family story, a heroic act, a sports article, a stranger's kindness, a child's determination, or an uplifting message on a simple television episode. We should find the good in things and let them uplift us. There are numerous motivating examples all around us. It is our decision   why we choose these examples and how much influence they will have in our lives.

We should always remember that no person is perfect no matter how great their story or accomplishments are. Even our heroes fall. We should not lose motivation when those we look up to fail. Better yet we can use it as a tool to further provoke us and bring us closer to the ideals and triumphs that have been achieved by our idols. As powerful and talented as many of our heroes may seem, they have all fallen victim to adversity. Even Superman has a weakness. If there is one thing that I know it is that life will knock you down. Follow the example of those that cherish the opportunity to get back up and persevere. There are many great people who accomplish great things every day. Use these achievements as a catalyst to push us toward our goals. No matter how limited we may feel, there are so many that have proven that even with the most extreme disabilities or circumstances, with a motivated and undeterred spirit, anyone who chooses to can achieve great things.

**Believe in yourself and all that you are.**

**Know that there is something inside you**

**that is greater than any obstacle.**

**-Christian D. Larson-**

## HOPE

**"Most of the important things in the world have been accomplished by people who have kept on trying when there seemed to be no hope at all." Dale Carnegie**

It has been said that hope is everything to a human being and without it we are lost. Some of us hope to be popular and successful. Many times we hope for material things. Other times we hope for better situations. Most people realize at a young age that eventually we must strive and work hard to make our hopes and dreams come true. The question I ask is "Do you have the ability and determination to remain inspired throughout all of life's ups and downs?" It is easy for us to get caught up in moments of inspiration and even easier to lose that stimulating desire. For all the things we might hope for there are those who hope and do all they must just to survive another day. Know that each day is a blessing and brings chance. Take full advantage and seek out every opportunity. Hope for the best and prepare for the worst. Remember don't just have hope for what may be easy. Accept life's challenges and hope to endure all things.

**-Do something today that will help you accomplish your hopes for the future.-**

## Inspiration

" There are only two ways to live your life. One as though nothing is a miracle. The other is as though everything is a miracle."
-Albert Einstein

Be inspired. Recognize the power of your emotions and raise your intellect. The world can be a very cruel place. Its every day pressures and influence can sometimes dim our lights from within. Sometimes we need to stop listening to all the racket of the world and follow where our hearts take us. Many times, our greatest and most simple sources of inspiration come, from inside of us. Educate yourself through every outlet available. Seek out positive and great things. Use your inspiration for good. As much as others inspire you, be an example to yourself and help raise the spirits of others. Listen to that still small voice and most likely it will guide you and help you with just about all the inspiration you may need.

"Never allow anyone to rain on your parade and thus cast a pall of gloom and defeat on the entire day. Remember that no talent, no self-denial, no brains, no character, are required to set up in the fault-finding business. Nothing external can have any power over you unless you permit it. Your time is too precious to be sacrificed in wasted days combating the menial forces of hate, jealously, and envy. Guard your fragile life carefully. Only God can shape a flower, but any foolish child can pull it to pieces."
-Og Mandino

"I'd rather be a could-be if I cannot be an are; because a could-be is a maybe who is reaching for a star. I'd rather be a has-been than a might-have-been, by far; for a might have-been has never been, but a has was once an are."
-Milton Berle

## Let Your Writing Serve As a Source of Inspiration

One of my best investments was taking time to maintain a journal. I encourage others to make time to develop a relationship with your thoughts through detailed writing. Imagine all the inspiring ideas, uplifting moments, and motivational experiences that get buried away in lost memories. Who better to learn and relate to than ourselves? It can be so uplifting when reading of past trials, remembering how difficult things may have seemed at the time and how strong you have become in spite of them. Sometimes it becomes rewarding to read of our past accomplishments. Many times we forgot how thoughtful and opinionated we might have been on certain subjects or ideas. Take the time to begin what may become your life's handbook of inspiration, understanding, and education. Start your journal off with an introduction about yourself and where you feel you are at this particular time in your life. Describe what you have been through and where you see yourself going. Make a list, a sort of guideline of what inspires you. Write what you want to accomplish and how you might go about doing so.

1. Who am I? Am I fulfilling my potential or am I settling for typical results?
2. What is my purpose? Do I truly believe in anything of meaning? What actions are necessary in order to enhance and share this purpose that I choose to stand for?
3. Who and what do I believe in? What are the principles and morals that help sculpt my character into being a better human being? Who are my idols? Why and how do I strive to be more like them?
4. What have I endured? Do I understand the growth and enlightenment that comes with overcoming adversity?
5. What am I searching for and what are my goals? Are my goals attainable? Do I have a strategy to achieve my aspirations?

6. What inspires me and what is my motivation? How do I recognize things that uplift and encourage my improvement? What moves me to take action toward my goals?

7. What are my abilities? Do I recognize the strengths and talents that I have been blessed with? Do I maximize the usage of my abilities or do they lie in slumber wasting potential?

8. What are my weaknesses? Do I have the ability to recognize my shortcomings, and what must I do to strengthen them?

9. How can I improve myself? Am I willing to become a better person? What must I do to be at my best?

10. What am I grateful for? Do I realize and take full advantage of all the blessings that accompany my life's journey? Am I appreciative of each day and the chance to participate in living?

Whenever possible, take time to read and reflect on your writings. Read of your past thoughts, daily activities, and life theories. Your writings are your ideas, understandings, and beliefs. Let your words be your inspiration to an improved journey. Gather all other forms of motivation and information. If a story or an article inspires you, make a copy for your journal. Write about why certain stories, and how the people involved, create such interest for you. It is your handbook. If you feel something is significant or a source of encouragement than by all means use it as you feel necessary. As you look back at all of your writings, discover the hidden gems of encouragement throughout your journal. You have a voice; use it as motivation.

"In an age of nothing, at a time when we stand at the brink of our own destruction?
Strengthen your belief in yourself, in the future of humanity, in the things of this world that cannot be easily perceived.
Awaken that which lies dormant now within your soul. Re-ignite the flame of your consciousness, and measure the strength of your conviction.
Reveal the lie.
Renounce your hatred.
Seek, find and embrace the truths you are fortunate enough to discover. Cherish them. Use them to anchor you in the sea of chaos that is the world we live in.
When twilight draws near, when you are pushed to the very limits of your soul, When it seems that all you have left are the dead remnants of the fabric of your life?
Believe."
**Unknown**

Sometimes we need to believe in something other than ourselves. Sometimes it may be the belief of not being able to let a loved one down. Maybe someone dear to you has passed away and you believe that you must accomplish some great goal in honor of his or her memory. Maybe you have children and you believe them to be all the inspiration you need. Maybe you believe in a cause or principle, its meaning and how it can help and affect others. Maybe it's a belief in your country or a gospel or a spiritual being. My advice to you is to make a choice to believe in something. You give a man something to believe in and that man becomes more powerful and determined than he ever was. Grab someone, something, some principle or moral that you believe in. Use ideals and beliefs that provoke positivity and develop and strengthen the good abilities you have within. Whatever it may be, believe that it can help get you through the most difficult times and inspire you to greatness. Also, believe in things that will keep you humbled and grounded through your achievements.

# " I am the greatest, I said that even before I knew I was."

## -Muhammad Ali

Believe with all your heart. If there is one single investment you can make, trust in yourself. Have a firm conviction in your abilities and let your effort erase any doubts you might have. Know that obstacles will be in your way and that life can be unfair at times. Still, believe with all your might that you can do it. You can be influenced by great people and wonderful ideals, but ultimately you will find that without self-motivation, belief in yourself, and the ability to take responsibility and action you will never be all you can. You have every tool and ability that is needed for your success deep within. Nobody is better than you when you are at your best. At our best, we are all equals; no one person better than the other. Believe in your ability to be everything that you can be. Know that you can and will achieve any and everything that your heart may desire. Let your determination and unbreakable will be an immovable force grinding its way toward achievement. Against all odds, believe in your capabilities. Believe in your purpose, ability to give maximum effort, and fortitude to persevere. Believe that you will not lose or fail throughout your endeavors. Believe that you are brave, bold, and talented enough to make your dreams come true.

**"Hello! You play to win the game!"**

**-Coach Herm Edwards**

**"All things are possible to them that believe. Surely we must believe in a thing before we can desire it; And God does grant unto men according to their desire."**
**Hartmann Rector Jr.**

I shared this quote on the Internet and was surprised by the amount of negative feedback that was given in response. Many of those who criticized were your average faith-bashing naysayers. Though I knew nothing good would probably come from my attempts to explain why I chose this quote to share, I still felt it necessary to share the importance of belief and the power of faith to some degree.

"All things are possible to them that believe? If you believe then I challenge you to walk to the moon!" This statement provoked my response where I felt it obvious to express what I was feeling at that time.

Dear Reader,

I am wondering if your question was rhetorical, or did you ask with intent of an answer? Also, if I may, was your challenge made for the purpose of mere humor or just pure disdain for the above shared quote? Is it not true that through the imagination, determination and belief of others everyday barriers of impossibilities are broken regularly? Wasn't the world once flat? Was it ever possible to think that we could fly? Has man not already walked on the moon? Obviously these theories were not proven wrong by simple belief and this is where I can appreciate your question and opposed stance. Still I must express my discomfort with the easy choice of so many to criticize and accept their own shortcomings rather than take the time and effort necessary to seek their own truths.

Of course belief itself is not the only factor in helping a baby take its first steps or giving those disabled physically the ability to persevere. Belief itself did not produce the paths and opportunities made available in rags to riches success stories. And it is not by belief alone that miracles are produced. However, my friend, this is truly what I believe. I believe that through most accomplishments and things that matter in this life you must believe first. Whether it is in your own abilities, relationships, business plans, or spiritual fortitude, you must believe first in order to make it work. Belief will bring purpose and if you have nothing to stand for you, might just fall for anything. **A strong belief will bring a firm desire, which can produce extreme effort, which may also lead to the opportunities necessary to achieve great success.**

Belief is not the end all solution; it is, however, the first and most important step of many down the road of fulfillment and a meaningful life. I choose to believe that anything is possible and that nothing is impossible. Our possibilities should have no limits, it should just be a matter of how much belief, determination, and hard work we are willing to exert. If you do not believe then that is your right. But why would you accept failure without giving it your all? Ask yourself what you believe in. Are you happy with that belief? Has that way of thinking brought you fulfillment and purpose? Believe what you must, but I am on a different path. I believe God does grant us by our desires because if we want it bad enough, he blesses us with the abilities  and determination to do whatever it takes to make our dreams come true; whether it be in this world or the next. He reveals truths about our desires that may have been lost to our own thoughts and actions. I believe because I have to. I believe I have no other choice.

## PERSPECTIVE

# "If the only tool you have is a hammer, you tend to see every problem as a nail."
# -Abraham Maslow

Who am I? What makes me special? What makes me better or more deserving than the next person? Perspective is a funny thing. On certain days, many of us sit and ponder about our lives. We reminisce about what we have been through and what we have overcome or achieved. We think about our failures and many times we dream of our wants and desires. For the most part, many of us believe we are owed something or deserve more. Now don't get me wrong, put me in a room with a certain group of people, and I could definitely feel justified in thinking I deserve a lot more than I might have at that time. However, put a different group of people in that room and that perspective might change dramatically. Where one moment I could have felt so under- privileged, the next group could have me feeling so humbled and grateful for what I do have. We can learn from others and their perceptions. We are surrounded by mysteries and complications. Many things we believe to be fact are just illusions of what we perceive to be reality. We should not lose interest in finding the understanding of things. We should seek the divine mystery in things. We have so many opportunities to educate ourselves and seek knowledge. We should do so with a responsibility to ourselves to find true perspective and meaning.

## UNDERSTANDING

**"Seek first to understand and then to be understood."**

**-Stephen Covey**

It's funny how our disabilities or restrictions sometimes broaden our ability to understand. A blind man understands that he needs a guide that helps him through his most routine of travels. Why do so many of us blessed with the physical ability to see lack such vision? Why are so many of us too stubborn to view things through the eyes of another? Many actions taken in this world are due to misunderstandings. Such misunderstandings like who, why, where, and how. It is better to admit a misunderstanding than to have animosity toward others and their beliefs because of a lack of knowledge. It is better to understand a little than to misunderstand a lot. Learning and experience are a process we must go through before we can gain a true understanding. Every day we should make an effort to understand things a little better than in days past. How can we love or hate anything if do not take time to understand its meaning or purpose?

**"Yet, taught by time, my heart has learned to glow for other's good, and melt at other's woe."**
**-Homer**

## PREPARE

**"Failing to prepare is preparing to fail."**

**- John Wooden**

You can never over prepare. Prepare for success. Prepare for failure. Instill in your mind that life is not always square or just. Do your absolute best to be prepared for the worst and unexpected. Always have a plan for the worst-case scenario. Have a back-up strategy for your back-up plan. Be prepared and ready. Many times when we look back at a mistake or missed opportunity, we find many deficiencies in how we might have prepared, performed, reacted, or made decisions concerning the matter. How we evolve from these situations bring true value to who we are and how we shape ourselves into the type of people we are looking to become. The true tragedy would be to face the same situations again and again and not be better prepared to succeed.

## PESEVERE

**"Hang in there. Hang in there because the greatest quarterbacks complete only six of 10 passes. The best basketball players make only 50% of their shots. The top oil companies, with all their geologists, drill 10 dry holes for every wet one. And even the most successful actors flunk 29 auditions for television commercials before they land one. So, *HANG IN THERE*."**
**-Unknown**

Whenever you fail at something, miss an opportunity or make a mistake, do not dwell on it. Definitely think about and analyze your actions and the situation. Don't, however, dwell on it with regret, anger, or sorrow. Use it as a chance to learn and gain understanding. Use it as motivation; turn it around and force it to have a positive effect. Work hard and smart and be prepared. If you can be better served to learn from others mistakes, use that advantage. If it is in your cards to learn the hard way, pay attention; gain a real and complete understanding. Don't take it personally, pity yourself, or ask "Why Me?" Learn and adapt. Grow as a person, gain perspective and understanding, and build character. Think of life's obstacles as a test. Conquer each challenge or keep trying until you do. Just do it. Failure is not an option. Never take no for an answer. Cherish the journey.

## PERFECTION

"I don't like these cold, precise, perfect people who, in order not to speak wrong, never speak at all, and in order not to do wrong, never do anything."

-Henry Ward Beecher

Choose righteousness and happiness no matter what your circumstances. So many times in our lives we hear the saying, "Well I'm not perfect" or "Nobody's perfect." And of course the saying is absolutely true. The problem with these expressions is that too many times we use the phrases as a crutch or an excuse to fail. The question is not if we are perfect. A better question would be, are we striving for perfection? Do we drive ourselves to be a perfect son or daughter, brother or sister, friend or companion, the same way an athlete tries to play the perfect game, throw the perfect pitch, or make the perfect catch? Pro athletes know throughout their careers that they will face failure on the grandest of stages and on numerous occasions yet the great ones cherish the opportunity to overcome the most challenging circumstances. We should always set positive long-term goals for ourselves. We should also look forward to the challenges of each day and do our diligence to be our very best one day at a time. Just as an athlete who has had a bad game strives to learn from his or her failure, we should use each day as an opportunity to learn, overcome our previous mistakes, and move forward towards our goals of being our very best.

"Perfection consists not in doing extraordinary things, but in doing ordinary things extraordinarily well."
-Angeliqyue Arnauld

## GOALS

Make a list of goals, short term and long term. Prioritize them if you like. Write yourself a summary of why you chose each goal. Specify each goal's meaning to you and how you think accomplishing each goal can or will affect your life. Now make a plan. Write down a plan for each goal and how you feel you can accomplish each plan. Try to put a time frame on them to set a standard and push yourself. Now you must make a choice to believe in yourself. Believe with all your heart, with no doubt in your mind that this is what you are going to do. You cannot expect others to believe in you if you do not believe in yourself.

## ACTION

**"Think like a man of action, and act like a man of thought."**
**-Henri Bergson**

The most difficult journeys begin with a single step. From small beginnings, great things are achieved. With every step you take, you are changing something. Aspire to make a positive change with each action you do. Too many times in our lives more is said and achieved in our thoughts than is actually done. We won't accomplish anything by saying what we mean to do. We can do great things if we choose to take action.

---

**To laugh is to risk appearing a fool,**
**To weep is to risk appearing sentimental**
**To reach out to another is to risk involvement,**
**To expose feelings is to risk exposing your true self**
**To place your ideas and dreams before a crowd is to risk their loss**
**To love is to risk not being loved in return,**
**To hope is to risk despair,**
**To try is to risk to failure.**
**But risks must be taken because the greatest hazard in life is to risk nothing.**
**The person who risks nothing, does nothing, has nothing is nothing.**
**He may avoid suffering and sorrow,**
**But he cannot learn, feel, change, grow or live.**
**Chained by his servitude he is a slave who has forfeited all freedom.**
**Only a person who risks is free.**

**-Unknown**

---

**JOURNAL-DO SOMETHING**

*Got to make a choice! Have to push. Have to press. Must persevere. How many days go by when you just can't wait to let an excuse throw you off track? You so passively give in. How many days go by where we do nothing to improve ourselves, whether it be physically, mentally, spiritually, financially, or in serving others? How many days do we do anything of significance or with any extra effort that helps us progress positively? As children we are so eager to learn, experience, and become stronger; we are so full of motivation, yet at some point we lose that light. Somehow, many of us lose that belief or faith in ourselves that we can conquer anything. Let's not blame reality. We make our reality.*

## <u>Journal-</u>

*I do, nothing*

*I can't stand the situation*

*Do not withstand the situation*

*With each day that I'm facing*

*I accept my situation*

# "I ain't play the hand I was dealt I changed my cards. I prayed to the skies and I changed my stars." -Kanye West

With so much opportunity available, we should never settle into mediocrity. I am no better than anyone else; however, when those that are close to you continue to fail and repeatedly ask for help, at times it can be irritating and sometimes becomes personal. It is definitely your life to live and you alone know what your pursuit of happiness consists of. Just do not be one of the individuals that mopes and groans about how life is unjust if you are not taking action to improve and succeed every day.

I know many that spend countless hours a day watching irrelevant television shows. It's understandable to relax and entertain yourself but don't complain about being unemployed when you spend countless hours watching reality TV. Please don't be like some individuals who spend time on social networks posting messages about their daily struggles, looking for attention and pity from the social network. It's almost comedic when you see the same person who posted of their unfair situation consistently posting about other useless daily activities. They announce how trying their lives are and how they are planning to improve the situation but later on post their destructive drinking habits at a friend's garage. How about those that put their financial status, or lack thereof, online and later you find them partying like a rock star at a local hot spot? How many concerts, parties, clubs, fight nights, or Vegas trips have you been too lately? How much money and time do you spend on video games, partying, or other extra-curricular, (key being extra) activities? How many days do you waste just hanging out doing nothing at all? How many jobs have you quit or lost for petty reasons? Don't get me wrong, sometimes we need to relax and release. Other times we need counsel and friendship. There are even times when we just need to wild out and have fun. The issue I have is that we should take responsibility for our actions before sulking about our situations. How are our choices effecting our positions and what effect does it have on others close to us. Who is making sacrifices to help us? What examples are we setting?

Many of us are free to do whatever we feel necessary. Well, what is necessary for your happiness? It is easy to be normal. Normal is easy. Don't, however, complain of a normal life without doing the things required in order to overcome normality. Look at yourself and ask; "Am I wasting time? Do I do the things necessary to achieve my goals? What can I do to improve my situation?" Average actions produce average outcomes, And remember average is just as close to the bottom as it is to the top. Be all you can be and take the actions needed to do so.

**"We have so many labor-saving devices today that we go broke keeping them repaired. Everything is easier, but requires greater maintenance."**
**-Lorne Sanny**

## A BEAUTIFUL MIND=No Limits

My uncle retells a story that he had heard concerning the power of our minds and how others take advantage of our doubts and can manipulate our beliefs. If told correctly, I believe the story takes place at a circus of some sort. A certain gentleman had a particular interest in the elephants and how such powerful animals were maintained. Upon first glance at those massive giants, the gentleman became distraught with an issue of safety and concern involving those enormous animals. "Excuse me! Excuse me!" the gentleman shouted. "How in the world are these gigantic specimens restrained with such a small rope?" The gentleman was referring to the rope that was tied around the right leg of each elephant connecting them to each post. The gentleman could not comprehend how such powerful creatures would be so passive and willingly restrained with no show of force against them. Why did they not have the urge to use their strength and will to break the fragile rope that holds them in place so easily?

The trainer later explained how, right from birth, the baby elephants are chained with large, heavy metal restraints. He also revealed that gradually throughout the years the trainers would use lesser restraints just strong enough to provide a firm resistance where the elephants' will to break the chains became almost nonexistent. That led to the point where these massive, powerful animals lost their belief in their own strength and had no desire to break free from any type of barrier whatsoever.

How many times in our lives do we limit ourselves from great opportunities because we have trained our minds to refrain from any sort of resistance or struggle? Obviously it can be honorable to practice restraint from certain activities and addictions in our lives. Still, it can be cowardly to not travel the path of perseverance just because the journey seems too difficult. We should train our minds with strong beliefs and determination rather than preparing ourselves to accept failure. Don't create excuses, because excuses do not reveal truth. Excuses are usually a way of guarding ourselves from our failures. We shouldn't let the outside world restrain us from reaching our potential. We must always believe in our ability to break free from any barriers that we may come across. The mind is our greatest tool and asset; strengthen it, don't waste it. Explore your thoughts, build endurance through will power, and strengthen your abilities and beliefs with understanding and education.

Don't be willing to give in or to accept defeat. Produce a will that shall provide you with the desire and fortitude to believe in your abilities to endure and overcome all things.

## What's Stopping You?

At some point you have to really ask yourself what's stopping you. What is stopping you from achieving your dreams? If you are honest enough to truly answer this question, the next question would be, is it worth it?" No matter how hard or disabling your obstacles may be, "Is it truly worth it to let your adversities win? Did you have horrible parents? So what! Did you grow up poor with fewer opportunities than others? So what! Have you been abused or neglected? So what! Nobody cares and neither should you. Are you going to sit and pout for the rest of your life looking for pity and handouts? You probably have a better chance winning the lottery. Better yet, you absolutely have a better chance eliminating your excuses and relentlessly pursuing your own success.

You can't change the past; however, are you working tirelessly to improve your future? Are you learning from your past? Are you provoking change in spite of it? You can't change previous mishaps, yet you can change how they affect you. Do your trials provoke motivation or surrender? Are you inspired to overcome or willing to gradually settle, justifying your shortcomings and always wondering what could have been? If you grew up around violence and selfishness, make a change. If you are surrounded by neglect and laziness, make a change. If all you know is poverty and limitation, make a change. It is easier said than done, right? Well, get over it; life is not fair and it is surely not easy. Let me alter the view point and say this: What if I said that you were weak, ignorant and that you would never amount to nothing? Would you accept what I said or would you be furious. Would you agree and share with me the excuses that will limit your progression or would you stand up and proclaim your commitment to proving me wrong? So why do we continuously look to let circumstance rationalize our failures?

I'm not being insensitive or unrealistic concerning certain obstacles placed in some of our lives; on the contrary, it is the exact opposite. I understand many suffer from illness, poverty, lack of education, the burden of supporting others, abusive relationships, violent neighborhoods, and so forth. Despite all the limitations that may be in your way, I absolutely believe that if you do your very best, persevere and strive vigorously to reach your goals, you will accomplish anything. There are children in the streets of war-torn countries, kids clothed with rags supporting themselves in slums all over the world. Girls are being kidnapped and violently abused everywhere, yet still there are miraculous stories of many overcoming such devastating predicaments by never quitting, continuously fighting, and making better lives. So what is our excuse? Don't wait for opportunity, make your opportunities and take advantage of them.

## Heroes and Work Ethic

**"It was about learning that there were choices and responsibilities. Now how are you going to make these choices? Are you going to stand on the corner waiting for somebody to give you something? Or are you going to earn it and deserve it so no one can say you took anything without earning it? I told him not to wait for anybody to give him anything. Work hard so when you get the gifts, they are yours."**

**-Mother of Michael Jordan**

Who are our heroes? What about them intrigues us? What draws us to them? Usually our heroes' possess' qualities and characteristics that we would like to share ourselves. We believe in them. We believe in their strengths. We relate to their flaws. We believe in their stories, their journeys, and who they have become. I think, most of all, we believe that with similar circumstances and faced with comparable situations we would triumph just as our heroes have. However, many of us faced with similar obstacles fail in comparison? Let's for conversation purposes compare ourselves with a star athlete. I like to compare sports a lot because a game of competition is a lot like the game of life. The raw emotions. The highs and lows. The chance of things being out of your control. Usually when you think of great athletes, you think of a high-skill level, and great physical attributes. You think of fame, money, and glory.

Imagine your favorite professional athlete and try to compare your lives. To make it a little more even, just pretend you are blessed with the exact same physical attributes that the athlete possess. Imagine how many people in this world play sports and the extreme work and sacrifice they put in to being successful. Now think about what small percentage actually make it. Compare their most difficult times. Imagine training so hard, sacrificing so much and then losing a fight, missing a game winning shot, or dropping a game winning catch. Imagine losing everything you know and have because of an injury. Imagine the unfair and ignorant criticism from those who have never walked in your shoes. Imagine being constantly traded from your home, moving to a new place to meet new people, and building new relationships. Imagine how many people, whether it is family members, friends, scammers, or bad investors, are trying so hard to get a piece of your hard-earned wealth. Now, imagine their determination to keep pushing.

I am definitely not feeling sorry for them, and I know many people go through much harder obstacles. Remember, they are not exempt from life's tragedies. My point is, how hard would we continue to work given many of these same circumstances? Obviously, there are many people that work extremely hard in the world; however, many people are lazy and content. We miss opportunities because we get too comfortable. We become dreamers instead of doers. We find excuses instead of solutions. We put more energy into criticizing and comparing our situations to others, rather than using that energy to overcome, evolve and create our own path of success.

People love to criticize athletes and say they are overpaid. It is my opinion that they have earned it and deserve every penny. When millions of people are trying to do what you do and you are one of the few that make it, you have accomplished a great thing. Athletes, movie stars, musicians- actually most people who are successful-are not just lucky. They put themselves in positions to receive good fortune. A lot of times they will their way to success.  Now ask yourself, do you spend more time dreaming or doing? Are you pro-active or re-active? Are you willing to do what it takes or are you content? We all have extra ordinary-talents; it's up to us to recognize our abilities and make a commitment to be our very best.

You can get so confused
that you'll start in to race
down long wiggled roads at a break-necking pace
and grind on for miles across weirdish wild space,
headed, I fear, toward a most useless place.
The Waiting Place...

...for people just waiting.
Waiting for a train to go
or a bus to come, or a plane to go
or the mail to come, or the rain to go
or the phone to ring, or the snow to snow
or waiting around for a Yes or a No
or waiting for their hair to grow.
Everyone is just waiting.

Waiting for the fish to bite
or waiting for wind to fly a kite
or waiting around for Friday night
or waiting, perhaps, for their Uncle Jake
or a pot to boil, or a Better Break
or a sting of pearls, or a pair of pants
or a wig with curls, or Another Chance.
Everyone is just waiting.

NO!
That's not for you!

Dr. Suess- Oh! The Places You'll Go.

## Talent and Effort

It's interesting to me when people talk of talent. They always talk about people blessed with physical tools, a tuned ear, keen eye, steady hands, great memory, enormous strength, etc. Many times in our lives we hear stories of people who, through certain circumstances overcame and triumphed through hard work and dedication. In other cases you hear of so many who failed because they gave up, or they just didn't work hard enough. You hear the phrase, "You can have all the tools in the world; however, if you don't have the heart or desire you are bound to fall short." I often debate with friends about how having heart, desire, and the ability to push and persevere through adversity is a talent in itself. Ponder that for a minute. In reality, most of us are lazy to an extent. We have an inability to motivate ourselves over long durations. We get distracted, tired and we find ways to justify our failures. My grandfather would always tell me, "No matter what you do, do your very best." See, we might not always be in control of the outcomes of things. However we can always be in control of our effort. In this life we're not always going to make the cut. Every day there are obstacles set up to help you fail. But I guarantee if every day you give your best effort, you will eventually succeed. If you continuously push hard, work smart, and give your overall best, those obstacles will become weak. "At some point, whenever the time is right, you will break through and conquer your battles. Remember, Rome wasn't built in a day. Sometimes it's not up to you to decide when you will succeed, but you can decide and be in control of your effort every moment of the way.

"I will act now. I will act now. I will act now. Henceforth, I will repeat these words each hour, each day, every day, until the words become as much a habit as my breathing, and the action which follows becomes as instinctive as the blinking of my eyelids. With these words I can condition my mind to perform every action necessary for my success. I will act now. I will repeat these words again and again and again. I will walk where failures fear to walk. I will work when failures seek rest. I will act now for now is all I have. Tomorrow is the day reserved for the labor of the lazy. I am not lazy. Tomorrow is the day when the failure will succeed. I am not a failure. I will act now. Success will not wait. If I delay, success will become wed to another and lost to me forever. This is the time. This is the place. I am the person." -Og Mandino

## DO IT

Success is not accidental. Achievement comes from developing the habit of hard work. There is an old Chinese proverb that says, "A man grows most tired while standing still." Are you the person that stands there, quick to criticize, while becoming powerless to your thoughts of exhaustion? Maybe you're the person that refuses to stand still and relishes the chance to build character through your actions? Extremely hard work and effort make it possible for the average person to approach genius. What we may lack in ability and talent, we can make up for in endurance and performance.

Do not let excuses be your conqueror. Do not justify or make apologies for your shortcomings. Just do it! Believe you can! Know you can! If you get knocked down by life's misery, get back up and accept the challenge. Hard work is not a curse. How we choose to look at our labor can be. We should not drudge our actions. If our tasks are difficult, we can put effort into emerging out of those difficulties; and with the knowledge gained, we can improve our situations tremendously. Some victories can come easy and cheap. However, most victories of any worth are those achieved through hard work and extreme dedication.

# "What is a big shot, except a little shot that kept on shooting?"

## DREAMS

"Before your dreams can come true, you have to have those dreams."
**-Joyce Brothers**


"I have had dreams and I have had nightmares, but I have conquered my nightmares because of my dreams."

**-Jonas Salk**


Dream big dreams that help you envision what you will become. Dream with no limits, yet don't let dreams be your master. Great dreams can lead to great steps. Help turn your most productive dreams into goals for you to accomplish. Let us not be like some who dream of wonderful paths of adventure and accomplishment yet still wake up and follow the same dull, boring road to nowhere in particular. Use your dreams as a source of hope and inspiration. Just remember while you're dreaming that someone else is awake, working, and striving to accomplish his or her goals and aspirations. Remember, tomorrow waits for no man. The more days we choose to only dream, the more we lose focus with reality and what is needed to make our dreams come true.


"The moment of enlightenment is when a person's dreams of possibilities become images of probabilities."
**-Vic Braden**

## PLAY YOUR ROLE

Lose yourself in the moment; don't, however lose who you are throughout your journey. We all yearn to have that feeling of freedom. We work extremely hard and search profoundly for moments in which we believe there are no limits in what we can achieve. You know those scenes in movies where the perfect song is playing and a prelude to the perfect climax is achieved through a certain defining action? Those are the moments that make a great movie and the same can be said of a great life. We love those moments because they invoke massive amounts of emotion, and we somehow relate to or gain understanding of those situations tremendously. They help the story become believable and in many cases, achievable or educational.

In a great love story we feel compassion or sorrow when true love and the characters involved face constant adversity and seem incapable of overcoming certain obstacles in order to truly love one another unconditionally. We become elated and overjoyed when the subjects attain a special understanding and complete appreciation for love despite any wrongs that may have come between them. Our value of love becomes so clear in those moments of expression. In other movies we become so inspired by stories of perseverance, such as a boxer fighting the biggest fight of his career after being raised in poverty and adversity throughout his entire life. There are episodes when we feel the union between soldiers as they gain a brotherly bond that displays the extraordinary loyalty between human beings, and the ultimate sacrifice for one another against the worst of all scenarios. Against all odds, their belief and commitment that no one gets left behind touches our very souls. Other shows have us become enthused with scenes of a lawyer's commitment to truth and defending the honor of those oppressed. Despite the difficulty of the case and the power of the opposition, the lawyer's determination and will to fight for what's right, stimulates and awakens our very own will power.

All of our lives tell great stories, whether of suffering, boredom, underachievement, accomplishment, conquering, caring, service, sacrifice, etc. We might not be able to have the final cut or choose every particular role we might want to do; still, we can display our talents in every part we play and or direct. I would rather play a miserable role than none at all. A miserable role could lead to a better understanding of misery, which may also help develop my talents and promote growth. This could eventually open doors to other

41

opportunities that may have never been revealed had I not made the most out of a humble beginning.

Master your craft. Whatever role or scene you may be in, become a master at it. Own those feelings or actions for the time being. If you yearn for a bigger role or outcome, do your due diligence to progress and change. Parts of our destiny are always in our own hands. We can always control our beliefs and effort. Go for moments and roles that you believe in. Without belief there is no desire; with no desire one cannot persevere. Great roles and impactful moments always seem to find their way before those people who will their way closer to them. Put yourself in a position to experience the greatest moments one could ever wish for. Hopefully, through your acts and examples, others will want to be a part of your glorious story or it may motivate them to create their own influential masterpieces.

## CHANGE

"Here's to the crazy ones. The misfits. The rebels. The trouble-makers. The round heads in the square holes. The ones who see things differently.
They're not fond of rules. And they have no respect for the status-quo. You can quote them. Disagree with them. Glorify, or vilify them. But the only thing you can't do is ignore them. Because they change things. They push the human race forward. And while some may see them as the crazy ones, we see genius. Because the people who are crazy enough to think they can change the world
Are the ones who do."
- ***Apple Computer ad***

There is change and there is changing for the better. We should change for a meaning or purpose rather than just to be different. Many times people want to do things to help, but usually they don't want the risk of being first. Throughout history great people ahead of their time stood for change and progress. Many intelligent people continued to learn and improve through such changes. Too many, however, remain ignorant and set in their ways. Usually, out of stubbornness, it is these people who resist progress and withstand the evolution of others. We should never be arrogant enough to not openly question some of our choices and beliefs. I'm not saying we should doubt our morality, I just believe we are capable of so much more when we seek out growth and development.

It should never be okay to just give up on your beliefs. However, I believe it is okay to realize maybe those principles may no longer be what you believe in. A better man is willing to recognize mistakes yet still have a desire for improvement and a passion for finding his truth. I believe if we are not able to progress or alter our ways we become irrelevant. We remain stagnant and stuck in a world of normality. Life should be about taking steps every day to become better. Whether it is becoming a better leader, parent, friend, employee, student, or person in general, we cannot evolve if we are living through the mistakes of yesterday. Change sometimes is the end result of true learning. Truth never dies, though ignorance can be changed if we are willing to do so.

# RECOGNIZE-OVERCOME-EVOLVE

## ADVERSITY

### Don't You Quit

When things go wrong as they sometimes will
When the road you're trudging seems all up hill.
When funds are low and the debts are high.
And you want to smile, but you have to sigh.
When care is pressing you down a bit.
Rest, if you must, but don't you quit.
Life is queer with its twists and turns.
As everyone of us sometimes learns.
And many a failure turns about
When he might have won had he stuck it out.

Don't give up though the pace seems slow -
You may succeed with another blow.
Success is failure turned inside out -
The silver tint of the clouds of doubt.
And you never can tell how close you are.
It may be near when it seems so far:
So stick to the fight when you're hardest hit
It's when things seem worst that you must not quit.

*~author unknown*

Journal:- *The world is not fair. Be prepared for the worst and for your dreams to be shattered. It's funny how I always seem to ponder and re-evaluate my history and current lifestyle when negativity seems to surface. The adversary is strong and he knows my weaknesses; and no matter how much I lust or partake of these temporary pleasures, in the end they bring nothing but pain and more adversity.*

**"You see you wouldn't ask why the rose that grew from the concrete
had damaged petals. On the contrary, we would all celebrate its
tenacity. We would all love it's will to reach the sun.
Well, we are the rose - this is the concrete - and these are
my damaged petals. Don't ask me why, thank God, ask me
how!"**

**-Tupac Shakur**

Whether it's good, bad, friends, foes, nature, the world's influence, or our own sub-conscience, everyday someone, something, or some part of us is at a tug-of-war with our goals, dreams, and aspirations. It's the classic battle of good vs. evil. Every day we fight the good fight within ourselves. Are we capable of doing true good without knowledge of the bad that we might do? We should not fear our faults and failures. Instead we should listen to the courage in our hearts and accept the challenge to choose what's right. Remember, a stumble sometimes can prevent a fall and not everything against us comes to hurt us. Without winter the spring wouldn't be so pleasant. Without rain there would be no rainbow.

Why does a dog that is missing a leg continue to walk? How do people with no rewards in sight continue to work three or four jobs to barely support a family? How do families with such good in their hearts and actions have such terrible things done to them or their children? Why is it sometimes that the good die young? Spencer W. Kimball said, "If pain and sorrow and total punishment immediately followed the doing of evil, no soul would repeat misdeed. If joy and peace and rewards were instantaneously given the doer of good, there could be no evil—all would do good and not because of the rightness of doing good. There would be no test of strength, no development of character, no growth of powers, no free agency….. There would also be an absence of joy and success." Sometimes our life's journeys are not about winning. We fight for a chance to continue fighting. We fight for the opportunity to experience, grow, and become better people. We fight for the ability to do what is right.

**"I shall be telling this with a sigh**
**Somewhere ages and ages hence:**
**Two roads diverged in a wood, and I--**
**I took the one less traveled by,**
**And that has made all the difference"**

**...Robert Frost**

**JOURNAL:- Poems of Adversity**

## Questions

Why does negativity favor me? I wholeheartedly strive to be as genuine as I can be. However, negativity is persistent in testing my patience and pride. Conflict constantly tries to persuade my pain from inside. Do I succumb to the rage and inflict its pain upon my negative enemies? Or is opposition just an obstacle and positivity the key?

## *Choose the Light*

*On my own all Alone*

*Night is dark as Death*

*My Heart is so cold*

*Is there any good that's left?*

*I struggle for every breath*

*Do I choose Life or Death?*

*Do I choose Wrong or Right?*

*Consumed by Dark, yet still there is Light*

*Shine, Oh Shine this light of Mine*

*My struggle back is far*

*Still you guide my climb*

*You Help Light up my Darkness*

*Relentless Light of Mine*

## <u>Crybaby</u>

*Sometimes when I'm alone I cry*

*To, release the sorrow I am no longer willing to hide*

*If crying is for the weak*

*Then, I am not as mighty as I appear*

*For in the presence of others*

*I have not shed a tear*

<u>Journal Note:-</u> *"For every tear there's a smile."*

*"You may shoot me with your words,*
*You may cut me with your eyes,*
*You may kill me with your hatefulness,*
*But still, like air, I'll rise."*

**Still I Rise-Maya Angelou**

## Humorous story of intelligence and overcoming adversity

A lady takes her pet chihuahua with her on a safari holiday. Wandering too far one day the chihuahua gets lost in the bush, and soon encounters a very hungry looking leopard. The chihuahua realizes he's in trouble, but, noticing some fresh bones on the ground, he settles down to chew on them, with his back to the big cat. As the leopard is about to leap, the chihuahua smacks his lips and exclaims loudly, "Boy, that was one delicious leopard. I wonder if there are any more around here."

The leopard stops mid-stride, and slinks away into the trees.

"Phew," says the leopard, "that was close - that evil little dog nearly had me."

A monkey nearby sees everything and thinks he'll win a favor by putting the stupid leopard straight. The chihuahua sees the monkey go after the leopard, and guesses he might be up to no good.

When the leopard hears the monkey's story he feels angry at being made a fool, and offers the monkey a ride back to see him exact his revenge.

The little dog sees them approaching and fears the worse.

Thinking quickly, the little dog turns his back, pretends not to notice them, and when the pair are within earshot says aloud, "Now where's that monkey got to? I sent him ages ago to bring me another leopard..."
*~author unknown*

## Journal Entry-*WHY*

*Why am I so angry? Why do I feel so heavy, so pressured? I can't breathe. The weight on my chest and shoulder's is becoming overwhelming? Where is my guidance? Where is my support? Those that are supposed to love me are never around. They don't care, so I don't care. Who was supposed to teach and mold me? Why do I learn more from strangers than my own blood? Why is the system set up for my failure? Why don't others understand? How come no one cares? Why do so many wear costumes to disguise their selfish agendas? Why do they judge and criticize more than they understand and assist? Why do the people who are supposed to protect and serve us steal from and abuse us? Why do I have to pay for my mistakes when the people who enforce these laws have no accountability for their actions? Why* does evil win so many times? Why aren't things fair and just? Why are so many who are undeserving so blessed? Why do so many good people suffer? I don't consider myself a weak person by any means; however, at this time I feel so defeated. I feel that I should be so much more. I feel strung along. I feel barely blessed enough just to squeeze by. It's America, the land of opportunity, and yet so many millions who are just as qualified and deserving never win. So many good, deserving people strive so hard every day, and the majority of those same deserving people are abused and stepped on. Is this my life? Am I only a worker ant, just here to be here and play my part? What is my purpose and why is it so hard to find?

"Can't stop, won't stop." "Until the wheels fall off." "All out." "Go hard or go home." These are some of the sayings that have stood out to me in my life. How many people out there do I idolize or envy? Why do I wish to have their same success without the journey? Most of my heroes came up against overwhelming circumstances yet, somehow, someway, made a better life. There was no guarantee that their hard work would pay off, yet they continued to push. They became examples of perseverance and determination. Ever since I was young I wanted to be tough. Well, then why would I even think about quitting during tough times? I can't choose to be tough sometimes, that's a cowardly approach. If toughness is in my character, then I should accept my challenges and choose to overcome them. When I truly ponder my troubles I ask myself if I would have it any other way. Most of us take pride in the fact that we grew up in certain neighborhoods because they are associated with struggle. It's like our certified badge of honor. There's a level of respect that comes with overcoming adversity. I need to fight for the chance of a new day. Fight for the opportunity for more opportunities. I want to break this cycle. Others may have fought and have felt defeated. However, they left the door open for me and our struggle continues. I don't know why some things are the way they are or why some have so much. I do know that I can control my effort and resistance. I refuse to fail. I cannot accept quitting. If I do not reach all of my goals, I will pave the way for others to do so. I will not lose. I choose to continue fighting through all my battles and give my very best. All out, always, until the wheels fall off!

## FEAR

"According to legend, one day a man was wandering in the desert when he met Fear and Plague. They said they were on their way to a large city where they were going to kill 10,000 people. The man asked Plague if he was going to do all the work. Plague smiled and said, No, I'll only take care of a few hundred. I'll let my friend Fear do the rest."
**-Unknown**

Fear is a disease that eats at our souls, destroys logic, and makes us less human. People always make the wolf scarier than he truly is. Fear will always be involved in our lives in one form or another. Many of our most telling moments in our lives are first provoked or confronted by fear. What is more telling and significant are our choices and actions in the face of danger. Do we push forward regardless of the fear? Courage is the ability to be scared, face it head on, and overcome it. You will never erase the fear of losing, but you will get more comfortable challenging it. Desire things more and fear less. Hope, endure, and build courage. Believe in your abilities, confront your fears, and never let your doubts paralyze you from becoming great.

"As the ostrich when pursued hideth his head, but forgetteth his body; so do the fears of a coward expose him danger."

**-Akhenaton**

## DOUBT

**"There is nothing more dreadful than the habit of doubt. Doubt separates people. It is a poison that disintegrates friendships and
breaks up pleasant relations. It is a thorn that irritates and hurts; it is a sword that kills."
-Buddha**

      I've doubted and have been wary of many things in my life. Many times my suspicions were justifiable, and others times I have been proven wrong. I am a skeptic as a security measure to protect myself from life's deception and trickery. I know, like with anything else, if we consume ourselves with doubt it can ultimately lead to a resistance that limits our progression. If we doubt the good in others and the abilities within ourselves, we tend to find ourselves lost in a negative state of mind. Of course, we should not be naïve and reckless with our choices and decision making. However, we can use our doubts and fears as positive tools to seek things out. We cannot disprove stereotypes and doubts if we do not seek to do so. We can find education and even inspiration in finding truths. If I have doubts about myself, shouldn't I want to prove them wrong? Doubt is truth's shadow. Usually, where there is truth there is doubt, which will either excite someone to find it or encourage others to go away.

**"Doubt whom you will, but never yourself."
-Christian Nevell Bovee**

## Emotions

**"The only questions worth asking today are whether humans are going to have any emotions tomorrow, and what the quality of life will be if the answer is no."**
## -Lester Bangs

We should not restrict ourselves from experiencing feelings. Being able to be in tune with our emotions is part of being alive. We should cherish and share our good feelings. We should not be ashamed of having certain types of feelings. We should enjoy the task of understanding our feelings and why we have certain emotions. It becomes harder for us to find truth and inner peace if we do not deal with the many parts of us that need to be explored and understood. Many of us feel that it is a sign of weakness to have certain feelings. We would rather be emotionless and feel strong. But behind our actions lie our emotions. They provoke and inspire us. We cannot act responsibly if we are not aware of our feelings and how we have come to feel certain ways.

I used to be so enraged and full of anger. I felt as if everything was against me and that I always had to prove myself. I became so entrenched in my own hostility that I was becoming a mirror image of those that upset me initially. I was becoming exactly like those who I said I would never be like. See, when you live through anger it starts as a little fire that is mad at those who have burned you before. Well, that fire only grows and is fueled by emotions such as revenge, heartache, aggravation, and displeasure. Soon that fire destroys all other emotions that help you mediate your feelings, such as love, sensitivity and affection. You become less of who you are, it destroys all of your good characteristics, and becomes routine in your actions. We become blind and are not able to understand our actions. Well, luckily I realized how much this anger was destroying my life and how it was affecting those that I did care for. I had to make a choice about what was more important to me. The negative was overpowering me, and I was losing control. It's a constant struggle, but that's the responsibility I choose to bare. I want to share my good emotions with those who mean so much to me before I destroy myself. I imagine all of the positive things that I can be a part of if only I use that same amount of energy I used being angry all the time to make the right steps toward positivity.

"You can't expect to prevent negative feelings altogether. And you can't expect to experience positive feelings all the time. The Law of Emotional Choice directs us to acknowledge our feelings but also to refuse to get stuck in the negative ones."-**G.Anderson**

## Gossip

**"The idea of strictly minding our own business is moldy rubbish. Who could be so selfish?" –Myrtle Barker**

So many hate or despise gossip; however, so many others choose to invest so much time and energy being involved with it. We distort truths and justify bitter judgments by using useless gossip. We spread terrible lies and destroy reputations with unproven criticisms and stories. We should not speak of other's business for our own entertainment; and if we are, we should ask ourselves why are we doing so? Nobody likes to claim their involvement in gossip, yet so many enjoy participating in it. Most information people seek about others is none of their business in the first place. Secretly criticizing others is a cowardly act; we have no accountability for our conversations. How do we take back untrustworthy rumors and disheartening stories about others character and judgment? Simply said, if we have nothing nice or constructive to say, we probably should not say anything at all about others.

## GOSSIP STORY

A woman repeated a bit of gossip about a neighbor. Within a few days the whole community knew the story. The person it concerned was deeply hurt and offended. Later the woman responsible for spreading the rumor learned that it was completely untrue. She was very sorry and went to a wise old sage to find out what she could do to repair the damage.

"Go to the marketplace," he said, "and purchase a chicken, and have it killed. Then on your way home, pluck its feathers and drop them one by one along the road."

Although surprised by this advice, the woman did what she was told.

The next day the wise man said, "Now go and collect all those feathers you dropped yesterday and bring them back to me."

The woman followed the same road, but to her dismay, the wind had blown the feathers all away. After searching for hours, she returned with only three in her hand. "You see," said the old sage, "it's easy to drop them, but it's impossible to get them back. So it is with gossip. It doesn't take much to spread a rumor, but once you do, you can never completely undo the wrong."-Unknown

## JUDGING-

"When you judge another, you do not define them, you define yourself."
-Wayne Dyer

Many times in my life I've questioned the characteristics, actions, and intentions of others. I dreaded those who I thought were racist, ignorant, hypocrites or just judgmental and fake. I guess, in fact, I was judging them just the same. For so long I was so quick to pass judgment on those I thought misunderstood me or my situation. Still I never really made any attempt to understand anybody other than myself. At some point I evolved out of my ignorance and found some humility in my life. From that point on, I've definitely tried to understand other's perspectives and situations. Of course, there have been times that I have fallen victim to a short temper or have been so stubborn that at certain moments I failed to focus or humble my heart in order to have a true, complete, or alternate understanding of how things may be or may have come to be. Still, I have come to realize just how different so many of us are and that different doesn't necessarily mean wrong. There are too many countries', cultures', religions', economic upbringings and physical abilities and disabilities; there are just so many factors involved in building one's character and beliefs that it would be unjust of me to ever pass judgment on anyone other than myself. Usually when we choose to judge it is out of ignorance, hatred, or jealousy. It has been said to not judge a man by his shoes because those shoes might not be his. We should realize the destruction and evil that comes from wrongly judging others. We should refrain from judging others and focus more on assisting and understanding one another. We can barely be trusted enough to make our own judgments. How then can we be expected to rightfully judge another?

"Everyone complains of the badness of his memory, but nobody of his judgment."

-Francois de la Rochefoucauld

"It is not the critic who counts, not the man who points out how the strong man stumbles or where the doer of deeds could have done them better. The credit belongs to the man who is actually in the arena, whose face is marred by dust and sweat and blood, who strives valiantly, who errs and comes short again and again because there is no effort without error and shortcomings, who knows the great devotion, who spends himself in a worthy cause, who at best knows in the end the high achievement of triumph and who at worst, if he fails while daring greatly, knows his place shall never be with those timid and cold souls who know neither victory nor defeat."

**Theodore Roosevelt**

# JOURNAL

*With great power comes greater responsibility. Greater responsibility brings more accountability.*

"Never underestimate the power of temptation to disarm your better senses. Throughout the ages good people surrendered their honor for the empty promise that wealth or power would bring fulfillment and their dignity, good name and self-esteem for the passing pleasures of sex and drugs."
-Michael Josephson

Isn't it much easier to stay out of a nasty situation than to get out of one? Our greatest triumphs and aspirations are in our minds. However, so are our greatest sins; we have an instinctive impulse and curiosity to indulge in temptation. Why then do we not train our minds to be tempted by good? Why not let our thoughts be consumed by positive activities? The more we are fascinated by achievement and accomplishment, the more we will be tempted to do what is necessary to attain success.

They say that it is weakness that makes us yield to temptation, but we must believe we have some great strength to endure the pain and consequences that come with partaking in sin. Truth is, we gain strength with our resistance. Opportunities are hard to come by; temptation will always be there. Desire to be great, not to be weak. Strive to achieve, not to barely escape the tragedies and setbacks that come with falling to repulsive acts.

## Laziness

If you don't have time to do it right the first time, how will you find time to fix your' mistakes? Many of us look for the opportunity to rest before we even get tired. We burn out our minds trying to find easier ways to substitute for effort and hard work. A lazy pace is surpassed by even an average effort. When we are lazy, not only do we fail, but the success of others is a constant reminder of how much more we can do. To live an easy life you usually have to work extremely hard. It's ironic because many of us can have the most inspiring dreams and as soon as we wake up we convince ourselves to go right back to sleep. We should definitely, when the time is right, rest and enjoy ourselves. However, when we are content and idle we are usually limiting ourselves from reaching our potential.

**"If a man will not work, he shall not eat."**
**-Bible**

What is the resistance that constantly influences us to rest from our efforts? They say that laziness is one of the devils greatest allies. Think about that for a minute. What is laziness? Being idle, inactive, passive, lethargic, unenergetic, neglectful, and negligent? These are all ways of describing someone who we might believe to be lazy. How would we describe someone who may be the exact opposite of lazy? Diligent, hardworking, active, vigorous, quick, and ready seem like accurate ways to characterize a person who we might say is not lazy in any sense of the word. Now, think about the two contrast of descriptions and ask yourself which category might you fall in more times than not.

I was watching an episode of a reality MMA show when a very talented individual was engaged in an argument with his coach about excuses. The coach, who was a world champion at the time was frustrated and fed up with the individuals constant complaining and his passive work ethic while training. The fighter, who had some legitimate issues with pain, would constantly find ways to make his way to the bathroom, stretch out a cramp, run for a water break, leave practice to see a doctor or tell the coaches of tender injuries that would affect how hard he would be able to go in training.

Now, those with a softer mentality might say that if the man is hurt, cut him some slack and give him a break. What harm would it cause to give him an extra break here and there especially if he was having some difficulties with his body? Since when does being hurt become being lazy? The coach doesn't know how hurt the fighter is and he might cause him more pain and suffering with such vigorous training methods.

Let's imagine what the hardworking, no excuse type mentality people might say about this situation. I could imagine most would argue that if the discomfort is so bad, then you might as well quit if you're not able to give you're all. They would say, so what if you get hurt. No pain, no gain. And that those who achieve great success are the ones who push through whatever obstacles are placed in their way, whether it is fair or not.

Well, the coach had an interesting and knowledgeable take on the situation and shared his thoughts with the fighter somewhat sternly. He said that when most fighters came in his gym, the first thing they said was "I'll do whatever it takes, no matter what, to be a champion." He then talked about the very small percentage of fighters who were actually committed to that frame of mind. He proclaimed how so many are always looking for an excuse or alternative route. He told the young man how he saw (quitting) so often in fights. How a fighter wouldn't make weight or, while losing, got disqualified for an illegal hit or sucker punched a guy at a news conference or tested positive for illegal substances. The coach told the young man those are actions of lazy cowards who knew that they had not done the work necessary in order to be their very best.

The coach grabbed the kid and asked him if he was a quitter or a worker. He told him if he couldn't push through the pain, then he was injured and needed to go home. He told him if he was not willing to quit (and give up his dream), then the pain was just exhaustion and weakness that needed to be turned into stamina and strength. "You got to pay the cost to be the boss young man." He told him there had been men who'd won championships while breaking their hands in the middle of fights. "Do you have that kind of mettle?" He then yelled and asked for the fighter to make a decision: either no more excuses or go home. "Go hard, give me everything you got, or go home." He went on to tell the fighter to give him his extreme effort when no one was around and not just when he felt all eyes were on him. He explained how discipline and effort breed the will of champions. The coach revealed the fighters words every time he was about to enter the ring for a fight. "I'm going to win this fight or I'm going out on a stretcher!" The coach explained that it was this mentality that had to be used each and every day and not just when it may be too late. That discipline and effort was the difference between those who made their way in this world and those who sat and wondered about what could have been.

Now let us ask ourselves, which type of frame of mind do we have and what actions best describe our efforts? What good is having dreams if we are not willing to put forth the effort needed to make those dreams come true? Do we deal in excuses or facts? Because the fact of the matter is that nobody cares about our adversities. Bad luck will either break you down or influence you to become the success you were always meant to be. In most cases life gives us just enough opportunity to make something of ourselves and never too many handouts where we do, nothing with ourselves.

"A chronic lack of pleasure, of any enjoyable, rewarding or stimulating experiences, produces a slow, gradual, day-by-day erosion of man's emotional vitality, which he may ignore or repress, but which is recorded by the relentless computer of his subconscious mechanism that registers an ebbing flow, then a trickle, then a few last drops of fuel--until the day when his inner motor stops and he wonders desperately why he has no desire to go on, unable to find any definable cause of his hopeless, chronic sense of exhaustion."

**-Ayn Rand**
***The Voice of Reason***

## CONSEQUENCE

There's a saying "Live today as if it is your last!" The reality is many of us are going to make it past tomorrow, the next day, and probably many days after that. If we are so lucky to do so, imagine the consequences that may stem from the actions taken by those who live today as if there is no tomorrow. Tomorrow brings accountability for yesterday's carelessness. Do not live today as your last day. Live today as your best day.

## JOURNAL

*I figured I'd just sit here and write whatever comes to mind. I'm grateful that I was raised in the church, because without it I would probably be dead or in jail. It's funny because no matter how bad I think I've had it at times, I know I have been truly blessed. There are so many unfortunate people in this world. It would be a shame if I did not feel privileged. I just wish my head was always as clear as it is now. How easily do I forget the things that should make me a better person? I mean, what do I really want in life? Success, fame, fortune? It would be nice, but is that what I strive for? When I know the true meaning of what I want, will I pursue it never-ending? So many times in my life my goals have been temporary or replaceable. Some of my failures could be blamed on others or circumstance. The real truth is I only fail when I give up. Nothing good comes without struggle. I know some struggle more than others; however, I am a true believer that the man above never gives us a load that we were not given the strength to overcome. Some of our greatest heroes have emerged from the biggest tragedies. I hope and pray that one day my positive thoughts become routine with my actions, and hopefully in the future I will be in a position to help others.*

## MAN IN THE MIRROR

Today was tough. A lot tougher than most. You know those days when the world is letting you know right from the beginning that no matter what you do it's just not going to be good enough? My heart is pounding, head is aching, stomach is turning and that is just right now while I am trying to relax and understand it all. So for now, I'm just going to sit here for a while and calm my nerves. I'm going to take deep breathes and tune out all the disruptive noises. I am not going to speak to anyone, but I am going to sit here quietly in front of my mirror and really ponder my existence. Sometimes we share so much of our time with others that we never really schedule moments of sharing and understanding with ourselves. We may even become dull to our thoughts because we are afraid of what truths about ourselves they might reveal. How can I truly fix anything if I don't take the time and have the awareness to fix myself first?

So I look at this mirror and I see a reflection. The room is dark and my heartbeat slows. I hear sad oldie tunes in my head. I feel alone and I feel tired. I feel beaten but not yet depressed. As I look at myself, I still contemplate how things happened and why. I need explanations and answers. I still am not willing to except defeat. My energy is low but now my mind starts to pick up. Why are these things happening to me? Is it a fair question? Is it the right question? Where do I begin?

Let's start this gathering of perspective by understanding who I've been up to this point in my life. Do I understand the people and their actions that have shaped some of my personality? Do I understand my character traits and are they coexistent with who I expect to be? I remember going through some horrible trials and witnessing very evil acts however I still manage to live. I also can recall wonderful times that I would not exchange for anything else that I might normally wish for. It is that glimpse of joy that reminds me, I did not feel so bad yesterday when I looked in this mirror. How many bad days am I willing to go through to enjoy a great one? The good times remind me that, through all the terrible tragedies in life, I have a choice on how I will let them affect me. Do I let life's beatings strengthen me or do I crumble in defeat? So I sit and I think I how have, made choices of character throughout my life using no excuses or rationalizations.

See, many days I feel strong and confident. I don't try to think about understanding my past because I don't care. I feel invincible. Life, however, has a funny way of humbling our spirits. You ever notice when things seem to be going too good life gives you a little slap in the face? Well, I feel that I've been getting slapped so many times because of my past transgressions. I have been on a steady road to improvement for some time now and it just seems that the harder I try, the more adversity grows. I feel like life is laughing at me for thinking I was going to get by unscathed.

Most of my life I considered myself a strong individual. I didn't care about many of life's injustices because it was normal. I wanted to struggle; but instead of using it as motivation, I found myself using it as more of a crutch as I got older. I kind of excused my failures through the failures that I believed others laid upon me. For example, I never cried or cared that due to certain circumstances my father was not around much, however, in arguments about achievement and why I hadn't accomplished my goals, I would share my broken ladders of teaching and leadership compared to others. When I truly look in the mirror I start to really understand the layers of irresponsibility and efforts of not trying to be accountable for my own choices and development. I can't claim the accomplishment of overcoming a harden life and still use it as an excuse for why I cannot achieve my goals. Do I cry about the many days I was beaten and scolded, or do I realize how firm my inner strength became and how it enabled me to be unafraid of danger and gave me the fortitude to stand up for what I believe in my heart? I'm not justifying the abuse. I am, however, presenting how I developed an ability of firm endurance and spark from total negative actions placed upon me.

Someway, somehow I must understand that most things in this world are against me. Hopefully I can take on the attitude that these obstacles are just resistance training, conditioning myself for a bigger work. Sometimes life is so simple, and in a blink of an eye it becomes so complex. What happens when doing the wrong thing is actually what is right for that instance? Why do we feel so strongly about certain issues and later on feel so indifferent about our prior beliefs? I believe that is why we come up against so much adversity and resistance. Every day we can learn something new about ourselves and, some days we just rediscover hidden feelings that have been stored away. But what good is all this discovery and growth if we do not use it wisely?

If I gain strength throughout my troubles, how do I use that force throughout my every day actions? Do I become a bully, or can I become even more humbled by its power? Every action has a reaction and we all have a choice on how we will act. If I act irresponsibly, will I be able to recognize it? If so, will I be willing to change? Now that I have spent a great deal of time thinking about my life and my situations I find more of a focus realizing my effect on others. So, again, I look in this mirror, and I ask myself what is really important to me. I am nobody's savior, and I don't claim to be some great leader among men, but I started asking myself if I am a good person to others. I was recently in attendance at a funeral for a past youth leader of mine and felt such love and humility throughout the service. So many from so far gave great testimonies of this individual's constant service and his sturdy examples of honor and loyalty. I couldn't help but wonder to myself what kind of example will I leave behind and how will I be remembered? The truth could be very harsh and frightening for some of us.

The more I look in this mirror the more I become indulged in thought. There are so many topics that shape our lives and character. But it seems the more I try and the more subjects are addressed the more things become clearer on a broader scale. I realize that I don't know everything and I never will. Some things require faith and others require action. Some moments call for aggression and others need a more subtle approach. It's a journey that we choose to be a part of. Imagine the blank canvas of a newborn baby. How many failures will a newborn have before accomplishments are achieved? Breathing, walking, talking, and developing emotion. How overwhelming would the obstacles be if each child new exactly all the shortcomings and defeats that would take place in their lifetimes? Well, somewhere deep down inside, I believe that we all knew our path of resistance before we accepted this challenge. So it becomes clearer to me that I should never speak of any hindrance as a handicap because I know that, since the beginning, I chose to endure. I will use each bump and hardship as a tool to broaden my perspective and help myself to become a better person.

I don't have it figured out, and I know I will be sitting in front of this mirror many times before my time is up and each time I hope I gain a little bit of wisdom and a little more endurance. The road is long, but I believe the destination to be greater. There is something bigger than me going on. How do I choose to be a part of that? I can only fight to be my best and do my best for others. I hope to share and give more than I want and desire. I hope days like this in front of my mirror lead to a better understanding of my past and what is meant to be. I hope through it all I understand that I have a choice to make wonderful examples out of horrid situations. Because no matter how bad my day may have been, that man in the mirror wants another shot at a better one and opportunity is really all that anyone can truly ask for.

## Mr. Perfect Became A Victim of Pride

Mr. Perfect was my hero in every sense of the word. He was strong, intelligent, and he made it out of our humblest of beginnings to reach what I thought was the pinnacle of success: the NFL. By all accounts, Mr. Perfect had no business being on the highest stage of professional sports. My family moved to Compton California by way of Western Samoa in the late '70s and early '80s. C'mon now, Compton, California, in the '80s with no friends or history in the city, being the new kids on the block and can barely speak English. If that's not a set up for failure then please excuse my ignorance?

A large part of my family eventually made it to Westminster, California. There my grandparents, Eight of their children, my great grandmother, and, sometimes, I resided in our cozy two bedroom apartment across the street from our local chapel. A lot of visitors would come over, and on many occasions they would spend the night. Times were tough and yet, as I grew and traveled back and forth, it always seemed to me that there was a certain unity that was built up with an overwhelming effort and pride to have a better life for the entire family. I never got the sense of singular accomplishment. I had an undeniable feeling of love as a unit and sensed a passion of success for all.

Everyone made tremendous sacrifices, although some, at times, would eventually sneak out and partake of the world's tempting activities, and rightfully so. Well, somehow that unity began to divide. Some that received the benefits of other's labor seemed unappreciative and those that labored felt owed for their hardships.

In a time of enormous struggle and minimal success, Mr. Perfect emerged as the family's lottery ticket. As a kid I couldn't understand the numerous family quarrels, the changing of tones and mannerisms when speaking of certain individuals. "Well, if it wasn't for me, none of you would be here." "Who helped bring you to America?" "I did this on my own, none of you did my training for me!" "Who gave you a place to stay?" "Who did you come to when you were in need?" "Remember when I did this...?" So on and so on. There was less discussion about the unit and more emphasis placed on the individuals. All of a sudden there was a lot of capitol I's on the team.

Well, Mr. Perfect was by all means the chosen one. No disrespect to the significance and the importance of others and their sacrifices, but Mr. Perfect was the one to get the family over the hump. He had abilities that all of a sudden sky rocketed him from high school mediocrity to the kind of story local legends are made of. How did a chubby kid from Compton work himself into a starting position on varsity football? How did a kid from Westminster High School make All-County and get a Division 1 scholarship? How did an immigrant linebacker from San Diego State get Defensive Player of the Game in the Holiday Bowl? How does a guy who wasn't drafted make a career of ten strong years in the NFL? The answers to these questions are kind of a tell-all tale in a somewhat tragic story that has become a long chapter in my family's journey.

If you let Mr. Perfect tell it, it was all his hard work and determination that got him to the peaks of his glory. However, there was one moment during a certain time of adversity when I actually saw a chink in Mr. Perfect's armor. At a low point in his life, this strong man, who I've looked up to my whole life, turned to me with tears in his eyes and told me how he should have never accomplished the things he had. I'd never seen him so humble. He sounded as if he felt he was not worthy of his triumphs. It's funny, because of all his accomplishments I was always in awe of him, but it was at that moment when I loved and respected him the greatest. He was, for the first time in my eyes, normal and human like the rest of us. I believed his honesty and admired his humility. He stated to me how it was his Heavenly Father who had helped him get to where he was and, if you looked at the facts, there was no other explanation. He stated how he let others fill his head and ego and how he started believing in his own abilities more than in his faith. I appreciated his journey and his spirit. The voice that he spoke with then was one of respect and love. I had never felt closer to him than at that time. To understand this moment, you have to understand my relationship with this individual.

I was a troublesome child, and in the middle of my high school years I moved to Orange County California to stay with my grandparents. My mother could no longer handle the burden of my negative actions and attitude. (That's a whole other book!) Mr. Perfect owned the house where my grandparents lived, and a couple young family members and I stayed there to go to school, work, and take care of my grandparents. Mr. Perfect was always around as the authority figure. I definitely learned a lot from Mr. Perfect. No other person in my immediate family on the West Coast had the education or experiences he had. No one could somewhat relate to the things I was going through as he could. Or so I thought. The more I respected and loved this man, the more he took advantage of and abused my loyalty. I started understanding other family members' displeasure with how he carried himself and looked down on others. In my own experience with him, I found that everything, and I mean everything, revolved around or related to him. "Man, who the hell is gonna fill my shoes?" "Who do think is gonna have to pay for your funeral?" "Do you know who I was chillin with today?" "I told you to do this because it involves what I got planned for you." "Do you know how embarrassing it is for me to go around the locker room and get shoes from the players to give to you guys?" "Do you know how humble I had to be to drive the blue monster (our old baby blue station wagon) to an NFL training camp?" Besides his one moment of humility I have never ever heard Mr. Perfect apologize for anything or display any admittance of wrong. That's why he is truly Mr. Perfect.

Don't get me wrong, he was a great motivator at times; but worse he was also a powerful manipulator and many times I felt he took pleasure in deceiving people. The more established he became, the more he used and looked down on people. More and more he believed his own lies, and more and more he overvalued his own worth. I was so grateful to get any type of athletic sneakers, but at the same time what sacrifice did he really make? So we got used athletes' sneakers even though he was sponsored by Nike and gave brand new pairs of shoes to his friends and acquaintances that would stop by. I am not unappreciative of anything. I am thankful for it all, the good and bad. It just saddens me how lies and deception ruined relationships that once were so united. We fell as a family before we really had a chance to start running.

It wasn't that Mr. Perfect was the only one wrong. The problem was that he was blessed with a greater opportunity to do a greater work. You can't claim to be the great one and not burden the responsibilities that come with the title. How, in your deepest of hearts, can you not want to help those that have helped you along the way? How can you not want to do the right thing? In our culture it is fundamental to give money to the head of the household, especially for certain occasions (weddings, funerals, birthdays, etc.) I remember a certain situation came up and a certain someone was bragging about how much they put in. I knew I was not on that same level of capability or generosity, but I knew one thing, I gave everything I had.

71

I just couldn't understand why someone who knew he was superior had to belittle the efforts of those who were on his side.

As time passed and as Mr. Perfect's value diminished mostly through selfish acts and ignorance, I saw a true fall from grace. I guess that's why building character and having faith in a higher value are so important. Who keeps you steady when the road gets a little shaky? Who reminds you of life's values and importance? Who stops you from your own greed? How can someone help you if you are not willing to listen? When you live a lie for so long, sometimes it is hard to separate fiction from reality. It becomes ever so difficult to separate your capabilities from your shortcomings. You lose your identity and purpose. Most importantly many times you end up losing those that you were originally fighting for to share life's rewards with.

I learned so much from family quarrels. I know many thought I was never going to amount to anything. It is not my goal to prove anything to anyone. I'm not trying to be better than anybody else or fix the mistakes of others. I am, however, trying to learn from others and our past. If I don't help make a change, then I fail my generation. I'm trying to be the best me I can be. I want us to be able to appreciate each other and do things for one another because it is what's right. No motives, no agenda, no expectations. I want to be there for you because I love you, bottom line. I have seen how jealousy and envy can kill the purest of motives. I know the farther away you get from your foundation, it becomes easier for you to break. I've seen how ego and pride can devour the strongest of men and lead them down a road of emptiness and pity. I've seen those who were so successful fall from grace and afterward witnessed the pace of productivity from those they had stepped on earlier in the journey. Oh the emotions of the rabbit when he refuses to change and witnesses the turtle steadily pushing along upward passing the rabbit and his false bravado.

For me this is where my biggest disappointment in the story happens. See, Mr. Perfect had a second chance. An opportunity came that could really unify things among his brethren and also allow him to do very well. I truly believe that we all deserve second chances. Some deserve more chances than others. The problem I have is remembering that day when Mr. Perfect acknowledged his mistakes and seemed genuine in making things better. What a sad time to have all the knowledge of your previous mistakes, and then be blessed enough to have another chance at doing the right thing in a similar situation and once again choose a path of selfishness and denial. How do you justify and live with greed? I don't blame Mr. Perfect for the family's failures. I just find it ironic that now in his time of need he has overwhelming expectations and criticisms of those he feels should be in a position to help him. I don't think he realizes that if he'd acted more loving and gave without expectations, how those he loved would have been in better positions to help and protect their brother in a time of need.

Mr. Perfect knows there was a time when I, and many others would have walked through fire for him. Every man is his own and we all choose our path. I just hope many of us realize we are instruments in a higher purpose. I truly believe we are here to help and love one another. Those who have greater blessings should believe they have a greater responsibility. Wasted talent is the purest of tragedies. Wasted service is a crime in itself. It is not our responsibility to expect handouts or success from anyone other than ourselves. It is our responsibility to reach our fullest potential and help others do so as well. It can be said that it is the fault of the giver if he gives what others have the ability to do for themselves. However, when you're in a position of great prosperity, it should be instinctive to want to ease the unfortunate struggles of others, especially those close and dear to you.

As I continue to grow and fight for a better future, I hope and pray that I have truly learned from the example of others. It's easy to say what you would have done in similar situations. You hope to work on yourself enough to where you truly trust your judgment. I never want to be one that gets swallowed up by my own pride. I don't want to succumb to life's evils such as greed and selfishness. I hope that I am able to help others and serve those in need. I hope I find fulfillment in loving others. I pray that I am humble enough to know that no matter how hard I work and what rewards I may receive there are so many who deserve service. I do not want to give and expect gratitude or loyalty. I just want to help because I want to use the good inside of me. When you act out of a loving heart, despite any outcome that may develop, in the long run life will find a way to make things right. Thank you, Mr. Perfect for all of your examples. I hope to use our past as a history lesson to improve and evolve and to bring out our very best from within.

# BUILDING CHARACTER

# &

# CONTINUOUS IMPROVEMENT

## CHARACTER

Our effort should be in building character and not reputation. Character is who we are. Reputation is what people say we are. Character consists of the presence or lack of virtue, honesty, courage, loyalty, and integrity. Build good character. Have pride in being a good person. Have honor in your name and existence. Choose the goodness within you and be trustworthy. Separate yourself from the negative and panicked; those are the same kinds of characters that look for quick rewards and easy exits. Be an example to yourself and others. Take responsibility and make a constant effort to choose what is right. Develop a strength from within that promotes honesty with yourself and prevents you from making excuses for your shortcomings. Have enough humility to recognize your weaknesses and be disciplined enough to improve on them.

---

An old Cherokee is teaching his grandson about life:
A fight is going on inside me, he said to the boy. It is a terrible fight and it is between two wolves. One is evil - he is anger, envy, sorrow, regret, greed, arrogance, self-pity, guilt, resentment, inferiority, lies, false pride, superiority, and ego. The other is good - he is joy, peace, love, hope, serenity, humility, kindness, benevolence, empathy, generosity, truth, compassion, and faith. This same fight is going on inside you - and inside every other person, too.
The grandson thought about it for a minute and then asked his grandfather, Which wolf will win?
The old Cherokee simply replied, The one you feed.
**-American Indian Proverb**

# If

If you can keep your head when all
about you
Are losing theirs and blaming it on
you;
If you can trust yourself when all
men doubt you,
But make allowance for their
doubting too;
If you can wait and not be tired by
waiting,
Or, being lied about, don't deal in
lies,
Or, being hated, don't give way to
hating,
And yet don't look too good, nor
talk too wise;

-Rudyad Kipling

## JOURNAL- BE A MAN

What does it mean to be a man? The dictionary defines man as a human being. But as a civilization, what are our expectations of a real man? Of course being strong and intelligent, being a provider and father are all synonymous with traditional descriptions of what a man should be. However, how can I become a better man without a better understanding of the perfect man? Society depicts man as a bully because a so called real man always gets his way. At a very young age we are taught through cartoons, sports, movies, etc. that the physically and mentally dominant ones are superior and winners. Is this truly our nature or more of our downfall?

For so long I wanted to be strong. Not only physically, but emotionally as well. I wanted to be hard in every sense of the word. As time passed, I found the people that I looked up to the most had very dangerous lifestyles. One by one the neighborhood tough guys were steadily falling to bad circumstances. Family tough guys were stuck in their past glory, regressing and eventually being replaced. They became angry at the world and anyone who came close to success. Many who had fast accomplishments and easy outcomes fell even faster than they rose to their peak positions. Many years I found were lost by those establishing the wrong reputation for the wrong reasons. How easy was it for actions by others to destroy the false prides of so many who lacked substance in their lives? I guess the more, life humbles you the more you reevaluate things and how you want to live. You find yourself searching for some sort of meaning.

I don't want to be like some of the people that I once looked up to who would not adapt or change. I want to learn and be a better person. I appreciate all I've learned from every person I've ever looked up to. However, I have to reassess who it is I model myself after and what kind of purpose am I looking for. A wise man once told me, "Act as if Jesus was with you." Now, this may seem extreme to some but what better example is there than the only man that I've ever been taught was the perfect man. How did Jesus handle gossip and jealousy? How did he handle male ego and bravado? How humble was he when dealing with those inferior?   Did he do what he believed must be done or did he question life's evils? Did he have mercy for the ignorant and those that despised him? Even if you don't believe in Jesus, you can appreciate his story. I found many times in my life that I should just stop, breathe, and ask myself what would I do if Jesus was here? Sometimes it never crosses my mind to think of him. But many times *the thought of him watching over me has saved me, from actions that might have eventually led to me kneeling down and praying for forgiveness. Actions I might have never done if I believed he was right there by my side.*

**"Show me the man you honor, and I will know what kind of a man you are. It shows me what your ideal of manhood is, and what kind of a man you long to be."**
**-Thomas Carlyle**

## **Building Good Characteristics**

1.  Love- Love with a pure heart. Love has nothing to do with what you are expecting to get, it has more to do with what you are expecting to give – which should be any and everything.
2.  Forgiveness-Forgiveness is love in its purest form. Compassion cures more than anger ever has.
3.  Patience- Patience is concentrated strength. You can chase a butterfly all day and not catch it. However, be still and patient and the butterfly will come to you
4.  Understanding- The key to understanding is the key to everything. We believe we know more than we truly understand. Don't judge others. Walk in their shoes to gain understanding and perspective.
5.  Humility- It is honorable to recognize our imperfections. Know that in the bigger picture we know nothing and can improve each and everyday
6.  Honesty- It is easier to be honest with others than with ourselves. Making the right choices is being honest with our spirit.
7.  Compassion- We make our best decisions when using compassion. Displaying compassion will lead to a better understanding of weakness, failure and adversity.
8.  Service- There are so many in this world who are in need of help. Don't just be, be somebody to anybody in need.
9.  Selflessness- You learn so much about yourself when helping others. Give to others as if today was the last day you may share with them. Give as if you believe, you have many days for your own wants in the future.
10. Thriftiness- Be wise with your earnings. Easy come easy go. Fast money leaves just as fast as it came. Don't let money and materialistic desires consume your thoughts.
11. Discipline-There are consequences if we do not discipline ourselves. Discipline encourages us to be responsible and respectful. With it, our lives become more focused and dedicated.
12. Effort- Determined effort breaks down resistance. Continuous effort unlocks our potential. The greater your effort the greater your story.
13. Knowledge-Investment in knowledge always pays the best interest. What you gain in education and perspective can never be taken away.
14. Kindness-Kindness is the language everyone understands. Kindness always makes a difference, for the giver and the receiver.
15. Faith-It's a lack of faith that makes people afraid. Believe in good things. Faith hope and love will always win.

"Let me tell you something you already know. The world ain't all sunshine and rainbows. It's a very mean and nasty place and I don't care how tough you are it will beat you to your knees and keep you there permanently if you let it. You, me, or nobody is gonna hit as hard as life. But it ain't about how hard ya hit. It's about how hard you can get hit and keep moving forward. How much you can take and keep moving forward. That's how winning is done! Now if you know what you're worth then go out and get what you're worth. But ya gotta be willing to take the hits, and not pointing fingers saying you ain't where you wanna be because of him, or her, or anybody! Cowards do that and that ain't you! You're better than that!"

-Rocky Balboa

## Coward

My father was in the military, and he got stationed in Vilseck, Germany. I was in seventh grade and did not want to leave California. There was an American high school on the base where we were stationed. At Vilseck, the junior and senior high's formed one joint education establishment. I was small for a seventh grader let alone a high school student. Still, inside of me was this burning fighting spirit. We came from San Pedro, but those kids were not familiar of the area. They did, however, have knowledge of Dr. Dre and Snoop Dogg, so I was comfortable claiming that I was from Long Beach. It was my first day of school. I had my UNLV gear on and couldn't wait to hit the courts at lunchtime. As soon as lunch arrived, I got to the courts and with a stern voice yelled "I got next!" Heads turned and the presence of the new kid in running rebel red with the cocky demeanor, was noted by many.

It was my turn and I got on the court and my confidence was booming. "Really" I ask myself. In my mind I was from the big bad West Side, Los Angeles, California, the land of Showtime and UCLA basketball. There was no way I was not getting mine on those courts that day. Those chumps didn't stand a chance in my mind. I stepped on the court and did my thing! Mouth's, were running, ankles were breaking, and egos were getting broken. Next thing I knew I'm face-to-face with the self-proclaimed starting junior varsity point guard. I saw through his false bravado. I sensed his hesitation and there was none on my part. We argued loudly and got physical. Next thing you know, Hand down, man down. I was smiling, he was bloody, and the courts were roaring! I just established my rep. I was oozing with confidence and through all the excitement, I started laughing at this nerdy individual trying to do the running man. "Wrong idea." The next thing I knew I was slammed against the fence and all eyes are on me.

How fast we can fall from soaring heights. See, the individual that I was laughing at lacked style and rhythm. What I failed to realize was how big and strong he was. He was probably a junior in high school and, though he had no rhythm, was built like an ox. There lay my dilemma. For all the cockiness I displayed, was I willing to take this as a loss without even putting up a fight?

Now I was the one hesitating, pondering in my head if it was really worth it. The excuses were there to justify somewhat of a punking. But what kind of person would I be if I only fought battles I knew I could win? This is far from a story about fighting and physical dominance or bullying. It is about character and when and where we display our true selves.

I knew what I had to do and we danced. Let's just say my pride took a huge hit, but I was able to walk home though I was well bruised and bloodied. I fought because I had to. What choice did I have? I couldn't be that kid who only gets mad when weaker guys push him. I didn't want to be like the parents I know who beat their children but when faced with conflict from their peers find a way to be civil and work things out. I didn't want to be that guy who works extremely hard when the boss is around and does nothing but steal when he leaves. It was about my choice of character. Physical violence in most cases is absolutely wrong. But to fight my equal for the pettiest of reasons and then submit to another because of fear would be cowardly and against the characteristics that I'd just displayed minutes ago. When our characteristics are true and not an act, our actions are routine and we don't have to worry about lying to ourselves and others.

## LEADERSHIP

**"The chief executive who knows his strengths and weaknesses as a leader is likely to be far more effective than the one who remains blind to them. He also is on the road to humility -- that priceless attitude of openness to life that can help a manager absorb mistakes, failures, or personal shortcomings."**
**-John Adair**

I remember when working for a large corporation I became unsettled with many who held management positions. I knew it was time for me to pursue a leadership role in the company. I knew I could make improvements in numerous aspects of productivity and work relations. Though at the time I only provided labor duties, I knew my work ethic and perspective of how efficient things could be done were valuable tools that would help in my progression. I knew at the time I was not the most qualified just from lack of experience on a management level. However, I knew that I could lead by example through my work ethic. I was willing and practical enough to know that I had much to learn from a leadership position. I also believed in my ability to relate to my co-workers and had a real understanding of how we could improve in certain areas. I knew there would be many who would not be comfortable with change and too many comfortable with previous methods.

I began my journey with an understanding of my position and how many superiors I still had to answer too. It wasn't about me showing how dominant and better I was. It was a journey to become a better leader. Each day I learned from both great and horrible managers. I avoided quarrels and also obeyed those that I had to. If I did not agree with my superiors, if warranted, I would communicate what I could when I believed it was possible. If I was in a position to just do as I was expected, then I did so to the best of my abilities. I would just educate myself on all the whys and hows. I would tell myself to get it done bottom line. Get it done at the very best of your capabilities. If it was not in my bosses' interest to change old procedures or policies, then I would work hard enough to be in positions to make those kinds of changes in the future. I never let my ego get in the way of my work.

If you are not in a leadership position, then don't just criticize those who are. Have the determination and the effort necessary to make a change. I once had an employee tell me, "What you guys do is easy! It's the BS that goes on that I don't want to deal with." Well, from my understanding that's a main part of being a leader, dealing with the BS You come in contact with so many different people and their personalities. You must know how to relate, motivate, and discipline in many different aspects. You have to know when to lead and when to follow. You have to know when to be humble and when to display confidence. You must be appreciative of others efforts and also demanding of it at times. You have to know of different experiences and how to produce the best outcomes. You must produce results and deal with rewards and losses evenly. Most of all you need to be an example of your very best and find ways to bring out the very best in others as well. Leadership is not about breaking people down. I believe it is about helping others realize their potential and letting them help you gain yours as well: We can learn from all people, all situations, and all things. It is up to us to determine how, when, and from what role we are in when learning such lessons.

**"A leader is a person you will follow to a place you wouldn't go by yourself."**
**-Joel A. Barker**

I have been subjected to many years, days, and hours full of bad leadership. I have been around egotistic, selfish, hypocritical, and controlling people who manipulate others more than they actually teach. I have been around some who could not careless about those that they are responsible for. I've seen false heroes with false stories who deceive others for their loyalty. I've known teachers who had no business being teachers. How can you become a teacher if you cannot stand children and are not socially constructive at all? How can I relate to you if you do not take the time to understand me? How can you use people for your pleasure or self-profit and not appreciate their service? The world is full of bullies. Still, for all the false direction I may have had, I would never say I was a victim to it. I survived it and became better and stronger because I overcame it. Would I have so much compassion for those oppressed if I had not had those experiences? Would I have such a desire to listen and communicate with the younger generation? Would I have learned of so many things not to do when dealing with others? Would I have the knowledge of what I expect out of leadership? I have so much that I expect from myself now because of the failures of others. I am a man who falls to life's obstacles constantly but I hope I have the awareness and ability to humble myself and the desire needed to improve and help others on their own roads to accomplishment. I just want us to learn and work together for good things. There are way too many bad examples of false authority in this world. I do not want to let them win by becoming exactly what they expect out of us absolutely nothing. They don't want us to be better. Their whole mind-state is focused only on their success and by all means necessary. I want to be the exact opposite. I want to help others rise to a place of kindness, sharing, appreciation, and teaching; a place of development and honesty. I want the responsibility of leadership because I want to do good. I don't want to criticize, I want to improve and make a change.

"Leadership is getting players to believe in you. If you tell a teammate you're ready to play as tough as you're able to, you'd better go out there and do it. Players will see right through a phony. And they can tell when you're not giving it all you've got. Leadership is diving for a loose ball, getting the crowd involved, getting other players involved. It's being able to take it as well as dish it out. That's the only way you're going to get respect from the players."
**-Larry Bird**

## Responsibility

**"The journey to happiness involves finding the courage to go down into ourselves and take responsibility for what's there: all of it."**
**-Richard Rohr**

It is in our nature to want to progress and evolve. As children we always wanted to be older and have more responsibility. Many times, though, we found ourselves not wanting to be accountable for our actions. We should always remember that with greater choices comes even greater responsibility. We should strive to make choices that promote growth and achievement, mentally, physically, and spiritually. The choices we make will help shape our lives and who we become. Every choice we make is our responsibility. Of course we will make mistakes along the way; however, we should put enormous effort in positioning ourselves into not making irresponsible mistakes that can produce life altering circumstances and consequences. Accept responsibility for your choices and actions. Your life will be what you make of it and no one else.

**"There are two primary choices in life: to accept conditions as they exist, or accept the responsibility for changing them."**
**-Denis Waitley**

## ACCOUNTIBILITY

Many believe we live in a time where most of us are not accountable for our actions. We tend to look for alibies and justifications for our mishaps because many times our egos and pride won't let us truly learn and grow from our mistakes. The problem with being comfortable about making excuses for our doings is that, eventually, we get lost in our reasoning. We lose sight of meaning and purpose. We do things for self-gratification and glory. We should be responsible for the talents we receive and the choices we make. We should choose to do good things because we know they are the right things to do.

## DISCIPLINE

I was watching a television special that featured a group of well established, very successful individuals and they spoke of their good fortune and how privileged they were to achieve such prosperity. They spoke of their undeterred determination to remain focused on their goals and dreams. They conversed about so many that they knew of or came across that they believed had such tremendous talent and how success seemed guaranteed for those individuals. As the discussion continued, they spoke of the reasons why so many so talented and full of ability never meet their true potential. The consensus that the majority came up with was that in most cases what separated those who achieve from those that underachieve was discipline or the lack thereof.

Think of the many people you may have known or heard of with exceptional abilities and promise. How many times have we heard of so many could haves, would haves in our lifetimes? We hear of so many victims. There are victims of excuses, substance abuse, self-ego, laziness, immaturity, and self-content. Sometimes what not to do is as important as what needs to be done. Discipline is the refining tool by which talent becomes ability. Discipline helps you to carry out your goals and keeps you on the right path. Discipline helps you become the best person you can be, not the one you could have been.

## Honesty

Honesty is the best policy. When we are honest we enjoy peace of mind. Others will do everything possible to deceive and manipulate us. It is our responsibility to not deceive ourselves or others. If we were to write our life stories would we be able to do so honestly? Let us earn respect by being honest with others. When presented with certain choices honesty can set you free. Truth ultimately prospers. Without honesty our ability to determine right from wrong becomes cloudy. We should not rationalize dishonest behavior. Let us not let the temporary relief from dishonesty fool us into believing that when there is no immediate consequence, cheating and lying are the right choice to make. Deception always resurfaces and many times it returns as a larger problem more complicated than before. When dishonesty becomes easy, you find yourself lying as a habit. You succumb to your lies and continue to do so even in the purist of moments. Respect yourself enough to be honest in your choices and doings. Let your truthful actions be an example of the courage and sacrifice it takes to be a person of honor.

**"Each time you are honest and conduct yourself with honesty, a success force will drive you toward greater success. Each time you lie, even with a little white lie, there are strong forces pushing you toward failure."**
**-Joseph Sugarman**

## PATIENCE

**"Have patience with all things, but chiefly have patience with yourself. Do not lose courage in considering your own imperfections, but instantly set about remedying them -- every day begin the task anew."**

**-St. Francis De Sales**

Many times in our lives our adversities, obstacles, and losses do more for our growth and education than we care to believe. It is usually our lack of patience that keeps us from recognizing the development that is taking place. There are so many instances where patience produces better outcomes rather than force. How many great things are produced suddenly? How many results suffer from quick actions rather than flourish through thorough ones? Can you count how many times where emotions and impatience caused you to think or act irrationally? It has been said that one moment of anger can destroy years of hard work and perseverance. We should not be in a hurry for tomorrow when there is so much we can learn from today. We should enjoy each day and all of its moments because the future has only one guarantee and that is, at some point in time our time will expire. So why are we in such a rush to get there?

## SACRIFICE

**"He who would accomplish little must sacrifice little; he who would achieve much must sacrifice much; he who would attain highly must sacrifice greatly."**
**-James Allen**

---

**Journal:- *Sacrifice What?***

*What am I willing to sacrifice? What do I consider to be a sacrifice? What am I willing to do to achieve my goals? Who are my sacrifices helping? Who do they truly benefit? Will I use intelligence in making my sacrifices? Do they have purpose? Are they for good things? Do I sacrifice with selfish intent? Do I truly believe in what I make sacrifices for?*

---

**"The men and women who have the right ideals... are those who have the courage to strive for the happiness which comes only with labor and effort and self-sacrifice, and those whose joy in life springs in part from power of work and sense of duty."**
**-Theodore Roosevelt**

When we sacrifice goodness we usually have consequences. Those that break the law end up sacrificing their potential and freedom. Why not use that energy for good things? We can sacrifice materialistic things that in reality serve no purpose or meaning for our quality of life and future success. Sacrificing for others builds character and brings forth a greater learning that can usually be learned through our actions of service.

**"To gain that which is worth having, it may be necessary to lose everything else."**
**-Bernadette Devlin**

## *Sacrifice*

There is a story told of a young boy whose older brother was in a car crash. The father approached the younger son shortly after the crash and said, "Son, if you will, you older brother needs a blood transfusion in order to live. The doctors have determined that only you can provide this blood . Will you provide blood for your brother so that he may live?" The younger son did not hesitate in answering he would indeed help his older brother. Unknown to the little boy was the relative simplicity and safety of the procedure.

The car ride to the hospital was unusually quiet for this normally very talkative little boy. The father, at the same time in the most awkward and difficult position of his entire life, thought best to leave the young boy to his own thoughts. The father and young boy entered the now familiar doors of the town hospital. As the father and son sat in the hospital room, the nurse entered with the needle in hand. She commented how courageous the young boy was, prepared the boys right arm as she had done to hundreds of other patients over the years, and slowly inserted the needle into his arm ; the vial began to quickly fill with the young boys blood. After the vial filled, the young boy, with tears in his eyes, turned to his father and asked, "Daddy, how long do *I now have* before I die?"

Unknown

## Service

You will not be able to do everything good in this world. The world however, needs you to do everything you can that is good. How many times a day do we act selfishly? Think of the many opportunities we have each day to provide service to others in some form or another. A friend or family member might need a ride. Someone might be struggling loading a large item into their vehicle. A broken down automobile might need a friendly push out of a busy street. A mother might be overwhelmed while shopping with her children and may need a door opened. Take time to think of friends and family, young and old, rich and poor, healthy and ill. How many times in our lives do we make an effort to call, write a letter, or send a card? How often do we ever take time out of our busy days to visit a family member or dear friend and say, "Hey, I love and appreciate you, and I want you to know that if you need anything, I'm here for you." So many times in our lives we take things so personally. However, the majority of us don't hold ourselves to those same expectations and standards. How many times have we written people off who might not have sent a birthday or Christmas card or was not there for an important event or could not help in a time of need? Service is selfless; it has everything to do with helping others, especially those in need, and nothing to do with ourselves, our egos, or our pride. Service is a remarkable thing, but it should be done with a pure heart and a free mind.

It is easier for us to find true happiness through service than in searching for our own selfish interests. If we live only for ourselves we will become bored with our actions and thoughts. If our minds are set on only ourselves and pursuing our aspirations, we may be blind to signs that may help warn us of failure. We can use service to uplift and inspire ourselves and others. Honest service is a true example of kindness and equality.

"I learned to GIVE

not because I

have much

But because

I know exactly

how it feels

to have NOTHING"

-Source Unknown

## I AM LEGEND

It's me against the world. Why not? Why have it any other way? Others lost hope. They believe our fates are predestined. They have not only lost hope but also their will to survive. There's a plague that is spreading. It's at war with our very existence. The disease is eating away at our very essence. It attacks our morals and beliefs. It is destroying our strength from within. Any meaning or purpose is eroding throughout the process of survival. Every day there are more casualties, souls are infected, and enormous potential is destroyed. Beautiful spirits become lifeless zombies. This world is surrounded by the walking dead.

There is great sadness in watching others become lifeless; especially when it is those that are dear to you who become numb to feelings of honor, merit, quality, and righteousness. They say the infected are too many, that we live in a time where self-interest is common interest. The common belief is that self-worth, greed, and obsession numb us from our natural instincts and ability to live in quality. How do you keep your head about you when all those around you are losing theirs? What is life without motivation and hope? What is life without that which is good?

Can I make a difference? I don't really have a choice of when I'm going to die. I can, however, decide how I am going to live. What lies behind and ahead of us are small matters compared to what lives within us. In the past, great warriors relished the opportunity of battle so that their names could be echoed throughout all eternity. I reject the notion of failure or asking for a way out. I accept the challenge of climbing the great wall of adversity. Even with dead souls and infected minds relentlessly pressing for ways to feed on my beliefs and destroy my spirit, I still cannot lose.

Light up the darkness. What is the powerful motive or great lesson that is to be learned from such a story of despair? What exactly is the meaning behind the cause? Survival. Is that it? Is it just the will to survive and triumph over extreme circumstances? To reap the rewards that follow the fame and admiration that come from such suffering? Sounds like a familiar story, though I believe it was the son with a less divine purpose that burdened the impossible journey.

See, at some point we became too self-absorbed. Our thoughts became dedicated to self-interest, our actions self-serving. That's how the disease spreads so rapidly without notice, because nobody cares unless it affects self. I cannot want to only survive for myself because my time will be up soon. My spirit will be sitting in the clouds watching the future of those that live on. Did I do for others? Did I do anything of service without selfish intent? When you are fighting for survival you truly realize how insignificant many of your past desires really are. Your heart and mind cherish the purest of moments and appreciate the goodness in others.

Do more for others than you would yourself. That's what I'm going with. That is what I choose. I am not going to complete this journey. My duty will fall short of the triumph. When this battle is won, I will be but a memory. Others will celebrate and very few will even know my name. But I will have helped. I will have done everything in my power to get others to the doorsteps of victory, and I will be overjoyed with their accomplishments. Somehow through the tragedy I found myself and what became important to me. What is important is to love one another. Light up the darkness! I am legend.

"The basic difference between an ordinary man and a warrior is that a warrior takes everything as a challenge, while an ordinary man takes everything either as a blessing or a curse."

-Don Juan

# THE BASICS

## EDUCATION

"Change does not necessarily assure progress, but progress implacably requires change. Education is essential to change, for education creates both new wants and the ability to satisfy them."
**-Henry S. Commager**

You can never gain enough knowledge or overeducate yourself. You should learn as much as you possibly can with every opportunity and experience. Your brain is your greatest tool in unlocking various doors and developing all the skills you will need to be successful. Just like anything in life, the more you apply yourself and take action, the better you become at it. I used to tell myself all the time that he or she was not so smart. I told myself they just had good study habits. I would be less than impressed with people who would drown themselves in literature or text. I would tell myself that they may be book smart, but they have no common sense or street smarts, no survival instincts if you will. This is certainly one perspective, and in many cases this may have been absolutely true. However, another perception and truth may be to understand that knowledge and education can never be taken from you and that the more knowledge and information you sustain, the better your chances are at success. Schools, books, and studying are not a complete education. However, they are a means to one.

"An education isn't how much you have committed to memory, or even how much you know. It's being able to differentiate between what you do know and what you don't. Its knowing where to go to find out what you need to know; and its knowing how to use the information you get."
**-William Feather**

When you see a true boxer vs. a brawler, the boxer displays his full arsenal of ability: his growth from experience, his patience, various punching methods, elusiveness, etc. You appreciate his overall skill set and how mental ability and dedication surpass pure physical talent. The same can be said for any expert at his craft. Most people that are successful possess' a great knowledge in what they do. Great quarterbacks play at a high level because they take the time to educate themselves about their team and play. They study each player's strengths and weaknesses and who they can rely on in certain situations. They study film on opposing defenses. They break down their habits and deficiencies and determine how they can expose their weaknesses. They certainly do not just go out to the practice field and work at throwing the ball hard. You have to work hard, but you must work smart and gain knowledge through effort and experience as well.

**"Education is the knowledge of how to use the whole of oneself. Many men use but one or two faculties out of the score with which they are endowed. A man is educated who knows how to make a tool of every faculty--how to open it, how to keep it sharp, and how to apply it to all practical purposes."**
**-Henry Ward Beecher**


## READ

I cannot stress the importance of reading enough. Though I believe experience is the ultimate tool when gaining true perspective and understanding, reading helps sharpen other important tools in our minds. Take the time to sit in silence and listen to your thoughts. Stimulate those thoughts with entertaining words from literature that promotes growth. I have been inspired by words written from individuals ranging from Tupac Shakur to Gandhi. I've learned lessons from children's books and have been reminded of principles and perseverance from the unlikeliest of authors. You wouldn't believe the parallels in lessons learned from a Spider-Man comic book and a spiritual motivational piece. As you read, unlock all of the many thoughts that remain hibernating without some sort of stimulation. If motivated, write down your thoughts; make a collection in a journal of some sort to remind you of your expanding abundance of knowledge. You will at times be astonished at the depth of your intellect, and sometimes you will find answers to questions you might be asking yourself. Have you ever heard the phrase "The answers are right in front of your face"? Whether it is a sports article about your favorite athlete, a book of poetry, or a Bible, pick up something and read. Enjoy your ability to consume knowledge and with it form your own opinions and conclusions.

## Humility in learning

"Humility is the only true wisdom by which we prepare our minds for all the possible changes of life."
-George Arliss

Be humble in your learning. A fool usually thinks himself to be wise, and the wise one more than often recognizes his foolishness. The longer our journey in life, the more we seem to understand that education is more than reading books or doing math. Education is above proving who is a superior debater or better problem solver. We should always find perspective in every experience, whether those moments are of joy or adversity. We should use anything and everything we can to gain understanding. Have your education prepare you for the opportunities and obstacles that may lie ahead. Do not use the knowledge you gain to diminish the significance of others. Educate your heart and soul with goodness. Use what you learn to help others. You are more influential than you think.

"I usually mess up, but I learn. I come back stronger. Everyone changes, becomes better people. We should all get that chance. I just want my chance. Whatever mistakes I made, I made out of ignorance, not out of disrespect. I was a reactionary. I want to grow. I want to be better. You grow. We all grow. We're made to grow. You either evolve or you disappear."

## R.I.P. TUPAC SHAKUR

## Simplicity

"Do you remember how slowly the days passed when you were a child? An 80-mile car trip seemed endless. It took forever for summer to come. When it finally did, by late-July, summer seemed interminable.
Basic arithmetic reveals that for a two-year old, the next year will represent 33% of her life thus far, whereas for a 19-year old, the next year represents 5%, and for a 39 year-old, only 2.5%...
More than anything else, the young child's perceptions influence how she experiences life. She has few markers that delineate the passage of time. On the first of each month, she pays no rent or mortgage. She has no job, and does not commute. She is likely to be regularly clothed, bathed, and cared for. The child arises each day with no agenda, no to do list. She experiences hunger, irritation, and sleepiness. She has some favorite activities -- her major activity is play. Each day brings new wonders... Meanwhile, she has no report to finish, no checkbook to balance, no across-town meetings. She does not even wear a watch.
Your life is a bit more complicated, and is related increasingly to how society has become more complex. Independent of who you are or what you do for a living, chances are that you're busy, perhaps extremely busy, and are a part of our active, generally hard-working population.
If you continually feel pressured, don't take it personally. You are experiencing the same dilemma as millions of other people, and you are part of the most time-pressed society of over-information and communication in history"
**-Jeff Davidson**

Many times things are not as difficult as they seem if we divide them into simple portions. Our heroes usually stand for simple principles like honesty, righteousness, honor, etc. As we strive for what we believe to be success, sometimes we lose sight of our most simple pleasures. Most of us have good health, comforting beds to rest on, and roofs over our heads. Many of our problems are because we complicate things with our emotions. We take too many things personally or become frustrated with stuff that has, no real bearing on the importance of our livelihood. Take a look at all that's negative in your life and see how much of it you can control by a simple choice of elimination. Addition by subtraction. You will be surprised by how enjoyable life can be when you simplify things and get your priorities in order.

## Communication

**"There is more than a verbal tie between the words common, community, and communication. Try the experiment of communicating, with fullness and accuracy, some experience to another, especially if it be somewhat complicated, and you will find your own attitude toward your experience changing."**
**-John Dewey**

Many times our ability to express an idea becomes more important than the idea itself. Unfortunately, too many of us have too many bad communication habits. Many of us build up walls or barriers to protect our ideas and thoughts from criticism or judgment. Sometimes we bottle up and are unwilling to communicate due to the fear of rejection. Other times we might feel that we just don't really have anything of significance to add or express. There are also those who are over confident with their ways of conversing with others. Some use their social strengths to belittle others. Also, there are those who speak through emotion, never realizing how their tones and mannerisms might have an effect on the people they come in contact with. Some like to get points across by not communicating at all, leaving others to try and figure out what they are feeling. For the most part, depending on who we were with and/or how we were feeling at the time, we probably have all used these different approaches of communication at one time or another.

Our message that we are trying to deliver should be clear in our minds before relaying it to others. When we communicate direction to others, we should be extremely specific in our requests. The magnitude of our clarity will have a direct impact on our desired results. How many times were you told to do a task and after you did exactly what was asked of you found yourself being scolded or punished because of some detail that was not asked of you was left undone. When I was younger, I was once told by an adult in our household to go to a house down the street and pick up some items that had been left on a front lawn for us to pick up. When I arrived home the adult came out and inspected the items and became very angry. The next thing I knew, I was being yelled at for bringing the junk home. I believe that I was told "Why didn't you use your common sense? How do you expect me to use any of this?" All of a sudden someone was communicating in such detail about how they would have never sent me to pick those things up if they had known the condition of the items. They were also very much full of emotion when doing so, I might add. I believe the first communication breakdown was during the adult's phone conversation when the person made the assumption about the quality of the items instead of asking for details. Second was the adult's miscommunication with me about the condition they expected those items to be in and what they expected of me if they were not. Third was the adult yelling and deferring blame to me and taking no accountability for her actions and direction in the whole situation. See how such a simple task when involved with such simple communications errors can easily become disastrous? How much energy, time, and emotion were wasted on a simple lack of communication skills?

We should have respect for ourselves and others when communicating. When possible we should avoid criticism, judgment, sarcasm, and demands toward others. When we speak with others we should speak openly and honestly. We should separate ourselves from life's distractions. We should try to listen and search for solutions rather than look to attack and give orders. I understand that at different moments in time when different types of communication abilities or methods might be better served than others. The ability to understand different people and how to handle different situations is a great skill that will develop with many opportunities if we choose to recognize and learn from them. As we learn and grow, I believe we recognize that we usually regret when we use negative methods in our dialogue with others. Usually it is after the demeaning words, broken trust, deceptive lies, or chosen silence that we sit and ponder in regret over how poorly we have communicated. In most cases encouragement, understanding, love, and trust, when used initially and frequently probably produce the greatest results possible.

Let us realize how our positive communication can have such a profound impact and example on others. We should never assume how another is feeling. If we are concerned or bothered by them, we should talk to them and discuss why we feel that way. If we do not agree with other's path of emotions, principles, or concepts, we do not have to follow or agree with them. It is our responsibility to accumulate knowledge and make our own way. Communication, like any powerful tool, can cause such damage and harm if used wrongly. It is our choice to use it to uplift, understand, counsel and inspire. We should choose to express love over hate and passion over anger. We should use it as a tool to strengthen, unite, teach, and learn from one another. We have abilities to sing, write, smile, and converse: we can communicate in so many various and opportune ways. Hopefully we choose to do so in the best of ways more frequently and most often.

**"I've noticed two things about men who get big salaries. They are men who, in conversation or in conference, are adaptable. They quickly get the other fellow's view. They are more eager to do this than to express their own ideas. Also, they state their own point of view convincingly."**

**–John Hallock**

## Time

**"The great dividing line between success and failure can be expressed in five words: I DID NOT HAVE TIME."**
**-Franklin Field**

One thing that can never be recycled or replaced is time. Each and everyday time takes away a piece of us that is gone forever. What do we do to affect the time we spend here each day? Today is a gift. That is why it is called the present. Master your time, do not become a slave to it. Be ready and take action. Do not keep your accomplishments waiting. Enjoy your moments in time and cherish the opportunities spent with those you love. Use your time wisely. Time is like money, we seem to forget its importance until we start losing it or feel that we don't have enough. How will we be remembered when our time has passed? Will we have accomplished anything of significance when our time expires? We should strive to make the most of our time and use the time wasted by others to help get ahead. Work hard, cherish and make wonderful moments, and make each day your masterpiece.

**"The best way to pay for a lovely moment is to enjoy it."**

**-Richard Bach**

## JOURNAL:- MOMENTS IN TIME

*Do I remember the moments that have accumulated over the years to make what is my life today? Do I remember what moment had the single most impact on who I am now? What was my most joyous moment? What was the worst? Did I cherish and savor those moments for what they were worth? I remember moments when I thought the whole world was watching or judging me. Then there were moments when I felt alone and invisible. There were single moments where I thought things could not get any better and there were moments when I thought I could not take anymore. I guess I could say moments are just that, periods in time and actions that have taken place to help me learn and progress. I should never get caught up in the moment or be in awe of it, because moments are just flashes in time when things are neither as good nor as bad as they seem. I should learn from each moment, whether it's a great one that helps me feel inspired to push forward, or it's one that creates adversity and humbles my soul. Hopefully with understanding I will try to create many wonderful moments for those that are dear to me.*

## TIME MANAGEMENT

Budget your time wisely! Make a timeline of things you want to accomplish. Make a list of things that you need to do on a daily basis. Prioritize your activities and put an emphasis on actions that produce positive results. Pinpoint wasted time and realize the wasted opportunities. Every day we should do something positive that improves us whether it is physically, mentally, or spiritually.

## LANGUAGE

**"It is still not enough for language to have clarity and content... it must also have a goal and an imperative. Otherwise from language we descend to chatter, from chatter to babble and from babble to confusion."**
**-Rene Daumal**

When I was younger, an old man took notice to the foul language I was using. He asked me simple questions like what school I went to and how old I was. He continued with a conservation that somehow got to a point where he stated, "Why are you limiting yourself?" He asked, "Why, with so much potential, would you confine yourself to such a restricting choice of vocabulary?" Right away I knew what he was getting at. It was just that I had never heard anyone talk to me about my language using such language. Usually if I got caught swearing, I would get slapped or beat up while getting cursed at myself. The old man really had me thinking about my language and how it represented who I was. He explained that when you use such words it shows others that you are too lazy or not educated enough to articulate your expressions except for those words used by ignorant individuals.

As a child I was always quick with my tongue, and now that I was paying attention to the language I used, I found great ability in the use of words. I would relish verbal altercations, especially with adults who would be so frustrated yet impressed with certain conversations that had taken place. I started really noticing the power of lyrics in songs and how poems could say so much with just a few commanding words. I became impressed with speakers and debaters who could display such power and passion without lifting a finger. I would be impressed with the character one might display by his simple choice of words.

I also found how devastating and hurtful words can be. I found how people deceive others with slick speeches and motives. I saw how vengeful and abusive people could be with words. I used to think that words could not hurt. It was just people having emotional reactions to those words, which was their choice. However, I've come to realize that we are all different and that whether you let them or not, words and language have a very profound effect on how we view and deal with things. Many concerns that I have known or felt were relayed to me through the words of others. Let's not just let our words entertain. Let us try to do great things with the language we learn and use. Let our words be tools of creativity and inspiration, ones of hope, encouragement and counsel. Let our words be a representation of who we are and what we are trying to accomplish. If we use great and kind words we never have to worry about anything negative coming out of our mouths. Remember, love is the greatest word in any language. If we use love for each other in our dialogue, we will never go wrong.

## Physical Health-

**"Money is the most envied, but the least enjoyed. Health is the most enjoyed, but the least envied."**
**-Charles Caleb Colton**

A healthy mind and body help us go against life's challenges. Day to day living can wear anyone out. We should choose to be as healthy as possible. Do not do things that set you up to become ill. Clean living is your best defense against sickness. Take great care of your body because your soul acts through it. If we are not disciplined enough to respect our own bodies, how much care can we have for anything else of significance? We must be weary of temporary pleasures that may bring grave and irreplaceable consequences. At times, when we are not careful, it becomes impossible to heal wounds of wrong choices we may make. Strive to make your outside presentation a reflection of your strength inside as well.

# SUBSTANCE & MEANING

## LOVE

**"We are not commanded (or forbidden) to love our mates, our children, our friends, our country because such affections come naturally to us and are good in themselves, although we may corrupt them. We are commanded to love our neighbor because our natural attitude toward the other is one of either indifference or hostility."**
**-W.H. Auden**

"As I have loved you, love one another." What really matters without love? If we really look at what is important and of any worth in our lives, nothing else matters without love. Love enhances, love inspires, and love overcomes. Love yourself, love thy neighbor, and love your journey. When we have faith, develop our abilities, and act with love we can expect miracles and create masterpieces for ourselves and others.

Imagine your worst days, angriest moments, and the most disappointing times in your life. Remember feeling emotions of depression, hatred, and vengeance. Life at times will bring moments of discouragement, abandonment, and surrender. The evils that this world reveals can be disheartening and sometimes will demoralize our spirits. Throughout all our adversities, love can prevail if we choose to let it do so.

What is love? Is love an emotion, affection, or an attachment? Is it a virtue, an action, or a feeling? Is there love in all things? I'm not claiming to understand its totality or proclaim that I have experienced its full potential, but I have found what love means to me at this time in my life. When I was young I did not like the word love. I felt as though displaying love or compassion was showing weakness or vulnerability. Everyone who I had ever loved had lied, deceived, or betrayed me in one form or another. Well, after years of stubbornness and anger, I've come to realize that this is truly why love is so remarkable and the greatest of all gifts that we could ever possess. Love does not seek out only those who may deserve or desire its benefit. Love pursues all whether or not they are willing to give it or receive. See love is the greatest emotion one could ever experience; it's the most remarkable affection and produces the most unbreakable attachments. It is the purest of all virtues, and the most heroic of all actions. The word "love" is the greatest of all words and because of its worth, it is not easily defined. However, simply put, love at its best is better than anything that there is.

Love is our greatest educator. There are many times when I did not deserve love and affection from others, yet love still surfaced. Love has saved me from terrible actions and selfish causes. I have been humbled most by love, and I have gained great strength through it. I have witnessed the many different levels of love, such as the emotional closeness that is in family love, the platonic love that can be associated with friendship, and the devotion of a religious love. Love is an instinct that brings us closer together and helps us survive through life's menaces and treacheries.

Love is various, it is found in most things. There is the love of self-improvement and the love for material possessions. Some of us would love to live a certain status quo; others simply love the chance of each day and what lies ahead. The level of our love is what will ultimately define us. Do you love others more than your own self? Do you love yourself enough not to make irrational decisions that may derail your chances for a better life? Do you love your religion or family enough to trust their guidance and follow their teachings? What sacrifices might you make for love? Are you willing to give love unconditionally?

If you love yourself, prove it through your actions; do not abuse your life and the opportunities placed before you. If you have love for others, show them through service and kind acts; everyone needs to feel loved by others at some time or another. If you have love for certain religious beliefs and for a higher power, do your best to be an example of those teachings.

In everything that is good love exists, but without love there exists no such good. Every time you experience an act of forgiveness, that is love. Every time you become inspired and are full of positive emotion, that is the power of love pushing you into the right direction. Every great person that you may have ever known or studied had a desire and spirit full of love inside of him or her. We don't all possess the same skill sets and talents, yet we all have the ability to carry love in our hearts and display it through our actions. When all else is failing, we tend to realize how much love helps us prevail. Love is like money in a sense: when it is lacking we start to truly realize its importance. Without love, nothing really matters at all.

Love is the greatest equalizer; it erases hate, ignorance, and prejudice. With love comes a greater sense of service toward one another, less thinking of our own wants and more reaching out to others. Love is the innocence of children, the energy of youth, the strength of marriage, and the ray of hope that shines throughout our adversities. If we love purely with all our heart, mind, and soul, love will conquer all and create a masterpiece that will be a great life for ourselves and others. Let love be our guide and bring peace to our hearts throughout our journey. Let our kindness be an example and may we share more love than hate in our lives and with others. Love is good. All the time.

## *"Love is the immortal flow of energy that nourishes, extends and preserves. Its eternal goal is life."*

## *Smiley Blanton*

## A Definition of Unconditional Love

## Written by Sandy Stevenson

I love as you are as you seek to find your own special way to relate to the world, or the way your feel that is right for you. It is important that you are the person you want to be and not someone that I or others think you should be.

I realize that I cannot know what is best for you although perhaps sometimes I think I do. I've not been where you have been, viewing life from that angle you have, I do not know what you chosen to learn how you have chosen to learn it with whom or in what time period. I have not walked life looking through your eyes so how can
I know what you need.

I allow you to be in the world without a thought or word  of judgment from me about the deeds you undertake.

I see no error in the things you say and do, in this place where I am. I see that there are many ways to perceive
And experience the different facets of our world. I allow without reservation the choices you make in each moment.

I make no judgment of this for if I were to deny you right to evolution than I would deny that right to myself and all others. To those who would choose a way I cannot walk, while'st I may not choose to add my power and my energy to this way, I will never deny you the gift of love that God has bestowed within me for all creation, as I love you so I shall be loved, as I sow, so I shall reap.

I allow you the universal right of free will to walk your own path, creating steps or to sit a while if that is what is right for you. I will make no judgment of these steps, whether they are large or small, nor light or heavy or that they lead up or down, for this is just my viewpoint. I see you do nothing and judge it to be unworthy and yet it may be that you bring great healing as you stand blessed by the light of God.

I cannot always see the higher picture of divine order. For it is the inalienable right of all life to choose their own evolution and with great love I acknowledge you right to determine your future. In humility I bow to the realization that the way I see is best for me does not have to mean that it is also right for you. I know that you are led as I am following the inner excitement to know your own path.

I know that the many races, religions, customs, nationalities and beliefs within our world bring us great richness and allow us the benefit of teachings of such diverseness. I know we each learn in our own unique way in order to bring that love and wisdom back to the whole. I know that is there were only one way to do something, there would need to be only one person. I will not only love you if you behave in a way I think you should, or believe in those things I believe in, I understand you are truly my brother and sister though you may have been born in a different place and believe in another God than I.

The love I feel is for all of Gods world I know that every living thing is part of God and I feel a love deep with every person, and all tree, and the flower, every bird, river, ocean and for all the creatures in all the world. I live my life in loving service being the best me I can becoming wiser in the perfection of divine truth becoming happiest in the joy of unconditional love.

**FAITH**

**JOURNAL:- EMPTY FAITH**

*I have been on this earth for twenty some years now. As I move forward, I continuously ponder and search for my own identity and meaning. As a child I remember being so very curious, sometimes naïve and impressionable. Just like m any (most) kids, I had an enormous imagination and saw myself achieving many wonderful things. However, as a kid up until now, temptation and trouble have seemed to get the best of me. Though my childhood was far from perfect, I am grateful for what I've seen and experienced. It has given me knowledge from many different aspects and helped me become well balanced in my own beliefs and judgments. I am thankful for a spiritual foundation. Though I would never deny my faith, I have not been accurate and obedient in following those teachings. I believe my life has fallen short of its potential up to this point because I have become distant with the principles I've been taught. I've become consumed with the ways of the world and its possessions. I settle for less because of my comfort level and my fear of failure. I settle for less because deep within I fear my theory of success and my ability to succeed. Sometimes I fear who I might become. Is it who I want to become? Will I have the ability to recognize my errors and change?*

## TELL HIM

"Let me be patient, let me be kind Make me
unselfish without being blind Though I may
suffer, I'll envy it not And endure what comes,
'cause he's all that I got and tell him
Tell him I need him Tell him I love him And it'll
be alright
And tell him Tell him I need him Tell him I love
him It'll be alright"


-Lauryn Hill- Then Mis-Education of Lauryn Hill-
Tell Him

## My Prayer

My Dearest Most Kind Gracious Heavenly Father, I humbly pray to thee. I thank you for this wonderful day. I thank you for my physical strength and health. I am grateful for my family and friends. I thank thee for all the good people both past and present and for their good actions and examples. I am grateful for my savior, Jesus Christ, and his great sacrifice and for all his teachings. I am grateful for the Holy Spirit that helps guide me throughout my difficult journey my dear lord. I am so grateful for the many times that thou has lifted me up out of difficult situations. I am grateful for thy forgiveness and love. I am so thankful for each day and the opportunity it brings.

Dear Lord, I apologize for my lack of faith at times. Even with all the blessings that have been bestowed upon me, I sometimes question your love and existence. When times seem unbearable, I sometimes doubt instead of bringing myself closer to thee. I apologize for my mistakes both out of ignorance and some with bad intent. I don't know why I have such dark and selfish feelings at times, yet I know thou gives me the ability to grow and overcome. Please forgive me for my sins. I am so sorry, dear Lord, and I am scared of becoming distant from my beliefs and the good inside me.

Please, Heavenly Father, help me to be a better person. Help me to recognize the lessons and answers thou has placed before me. Give me the strength necessary to live with courage, discipline, and humility. Help me to serve others especially those in need. Help me to raise a loving family with good morals and a respect for life. Please help me to do everything possible to provide for my children and give them all the opportunities I can in order to improve their quality of life. If anything is most important, I pray for my children's safety and physical health. Help them to be their very best and to always help each other along the way. Please be with our loved ones both near and far away and may they be strong through any adversities that may come their way. Please, dear Lord, bless those struggling to do good, and also those who are ill or have disabilities. Please have thy spirit be with those in war, and the many that suffer in poverty. Please Father, especially bless the children. Many lack the support and guidance needed to survive and progress in this world. Please be with them. Please have mercy on all our mistakes and help us learn and grow from our experiences.

My dearest Heavenly Father, I believe in you. I want you to know that I choose to believe in your love and need you in my life. I love you, dear Father, and I am grateful for the opportunity to be here on this earth and experience life. I am grateful for every tear and every smile. Each day is a chance to grow and better myself, and I look forward to those opportunities both good and bad. I know deep in my heart that I need thee in all that I do. There is no alternative. I choose you. I love you, dear Lord, and will do my best to do thy will. I humbly pray these words to you in Jesus's name. Amen.


## Noise & Faith

What is faith to me? Is faith believing in what I have not yet seen? Is hope a belief of a better outcome without a guarantee? What is my faith and what do I hope for? If most of us possess faith, then why do we lack discipline? If many of us hope for the best, then why do so many believe in the worst? I was once told to fill my thoughts with goodness and love, and that the rest is just noise. It took some time and every man's interpretation can be different from the next; however, I've finally come to an understanding of how that phrase coincides with my faith and actions.

How many days do we wake up and tell ourselves how grateful we are for this new day and how we look forward to the opportunities and possibilities each day brings? I think for so many of us we fail to realize how ungrateful and negative our daily routines have become. How many of us have more bad things than good to say about our jobs? How many times do we find ourselves criticizing more than supporting or uplifting? Most people, when describing their lives, always begin by sharing their struggles and how hard times are or what adversities they have been through. How many people do you know who would rather share their thoughts of love, joy, and gratitude instead of complaining or searching for pity? Do you know that it is usually easier for others to describe a family member, classmate, or friend using negatives than using positives. Think about that. Think of the people around you, your favorite sports team, or your place of employment. Usually someway, somehow negative comments seem to find their way into our thoughts. In many cases it's not malicious, yet still it's unneeded noise. Remember the quote that I shared earlier? "Fill your thoughts with goodness and love, the rest is just noise." How much do we display through our actions or speak out of our mouths that is negative noise?

What does noise have to do with faith? Well it depends on what kind of faith you have and who you might have faith in. Think of your greatest goals and aspirations for your life. What principles do you believe in? Don't most things that we seek out or hope to endure consist of a core of good virtue and intent? When we do something with bad intentions or even when we make simple mistakes, don't we in some way feel that it's not right inside? If this is true, then why so many times in our lives do we choose to ignore the good voice or feelings from within only to act as if we knew no better on the outside? Is it in our destiny to be miserable and seek out the noise of this world?

How many times do people of faith look to whomever it is they believe in and ask for answers? Like a little child bothering our parents we constantly ask for answers. We seek instant responses to our questions, and we expect speedy solutions to our problems. Are we too weak and lazy to try and solve our own problems first? Maybe we are just too impatient or arrogant. Weak, lazy, impatient, and arrogant all sound like the noise of this world. Maybe we surround ourselves with so much noise that it becomes impossible for us to hear or find the answers that we are so desperately seeking. It could be that if we filled ourselves with goodness and love that it might just enhance our chances of finding the right answers to the right kind of questions.

We can do more good by being good than any other way. Of course we are going to have bad times in our lives, but they will most definitely help remind us of all that's good and worth living for. Be grateful, work hard, seek knowledge, gain perspective, serve others, and follow the goodness that is inside you. Have faith in yourself to be the best person you can be.

"Where faith is there is courage, there is fortitude, there is steadfastness and strength... Faith bestows that sublime courage that rises superior to the troubles and disappointments of life, that acknowledges no defeat except as a step to victory; that is strong to endure, patient to wait, and energetic to struggle... Light up, then, the lamp of faith in your heart... It will lead you safely through the mists of doubt and the black darkness of despair; along the narrow, thorny ways of sickness and sorrow, and over the treacherous places of temptation and uncertainty."
-James Allen

## KINDNESS

**"Kindness is a language the dumb can speak and the deaf can hear and understand."**
**-Christian Nevell Bovee**

No act of kindness, no matter how little is ever wasted. Most kind acts cost very little, yet their worth and effect can be massive. Kindness destroys ignorance, produces wisdom, and provokes forgiveness; and it can bring light in the darkest of places. Having the capacity to care and serve gives our lives significance and meaning. I have never had any trouble paying back a debt; however, I have had great difficulty trying to give back the value of kind gestures that have been bestowed upon me in my life. True kindness is given with no expectations. Many times we are quick to expect other's best, yet we become so full of excuses when the chance for us to display our service and love are presented. Take each and every opportunity to spread seeds of kindness upon others. You never know when, where, and how those seeds of love may blossom again. With all the adversity we may face, it takes a great desire and fortitude to be truly happy and an even greater effort and kindness to share that blessing with others.

**"The individual is capable of both great compassion and great indifference. He has it within his means to nourish the former and outgrow the latter."**
**-Norman Cousins**

## FORGIVENESS

**"They who forgive most shall be most forgiven."**
**-Josiah Bailey**

### Forgiving Others

I was sitting in church with my family when the topic of forgiveness was brought to our attention. The speaker revealed how one night while praying in his bedroom, he had a sort of revelation come to him. The gentleman spoke of how humbled and sorry he was for some mistakes he had made with a close friend. The speaker told of how regretful and ashamed he felt and how he repeatedly asked for mercy and for his friend's forgiveness. He then shared how he felt a spirit in the room that prompted him to sit in silence and listen. As he calmed himself and his thoughts became clearer, he came to an understanding and gained a new perspective on forgiveness and its value in his life.

The gentleman continued on about how previously in his life he was such a hot head, held many grudges, and was stubborn to a fault. He spoke of his anger and the irony of his unwillingness to forgive that led him to the actions that he now was so regretful for. He told of how meek he became while praying when a subtle voice asked, "How can you expect forgiveness when you are unwilling to display such compassion toward others?" The lesson of forgiveness that was given through that simple question has helped me reevaluate my tolerance level and ability to pardon others and to look past their mistakes.

How many days go by that we beg for forgiveness and how many times in our lives do we grant such mercy when it is in our power to do so? Many of us fail to understand the importance of forgiving others and its impact on our lives. If we do not extend forgiveness toward others, our lives can become consumed with anger and hard feelings. Previous wrongs can magnify as they accumulate and once-loving relationships can become damaged beyond repair. I have learned through my own experiences that more good has come from compassion than it ever has from revenge. Everyone makes mistakes; our ability to forgive and gain perspective from these past actions can have great influence on our futures. Forgive but don't forget; however, forget your ill will and negative feelings. Free yourself of negative burdens, such as anger, that limit your progress and cripple your ability to build healthy relationships.

# "Forgiveness does not change the past, but it does enlarge the future."
# -Paul Boese

### FINDING FORGIVENESS

Our mistakes in our lives can become heavy burdens. When we thoughtfully look at our lives, can we recognize the past actions that have limited our futures? Do we have sorrow for the mistakes we have made? Are we willing and able to eliminate these wrongs from our lives? Have we thought to restore all that we may have taken or damaged? The effects of our intentions, thoughts, and actions actively shape our experiences throughout our present and futures.

We should not dwell on our mistakes; we should seek forgiveness and grow from them. Every day that we are blessed with brings opportunity to start over again. At any time that we may feel lost or that we are traveling along a wrong path, we have the ability to get off that road and begin down a new one. We can find relief in eliminating unfulfilling, temporary pleasures and begin moving ourselves farther away from such obstacles. True repentance for our past mistakes will open many doors of possibility and opportunity in our lives.

Sometimes the steps of repentance can be difficult and painful. Yet, if done with a pure heart, they can produce peace of mind, self-respect, hope, and a renewed life with great opportunity. When we take the time and make an effort to listen, the spirit inside us will always know what to do. If we want true happiness, we must seek forgiveness and improve ourselves each and every day. Forgiveness brings comfort and knowledge that we are making an effort to be our best. Forgiveness provides the courage needed to confront our weaknesses and face our fears. We know that through repentance we can find peace and fulfillment in correcting our mistakes.

## A Letter Two My Unborn Child

Life is a dream to some and a struggle to most. But in my life when I close my eyes, I dream of you. When I can no longer go on, and I feel that there is absolutely nothing left for me to fight for, I close my heavy eyes. When my eyes are closed, I quiet all my thoughts and listen to my soul; my soul reveals to me your greatness and infinite potential. In my heart I know you will be blessed with the ability to do anything you may desire. I hope you know with all your heart how special you are. I pray for your protection and health, because I know how special you are to me. You are my everything, my greatest gift, and my deepest love.

I promise that everything I do, I now do for you. I can't imagine taking action without your future influencing my decisions. I promise to protect and teach you. I promise to love and forgive you. I promise to provide you with opportunities to succeed. I promise to be there for you through the good and bad times. Always I will be there for you. I promise to let you grow but to always have an influence on your choices as you do on mine. I hope to never let you down; and when I do make mistakes, I will be humble and honest enough to take responsibility for my actions and explain to you why and how we can learn from my faults. I want you to understand that this world can be a cruel place, but it is full of angels like you who are put here to bring light to the dark. You will have a light that others will try to damage, but you are strong and smart enough to avoid, and when necessary, overcome the opposition with great strength.

I am so grateful for your life and will cherish every moment I have with you. I am proud that you are mine and I am proud of what you will become. Life will be very tough at times. You will question your efforts and beliefs; you will change and evolve both on the inside and out. If I could give you any advice that I would want to stay with you throughout your journey of growth it would be to absolutely under no circumstances, never ever give up!!!! Life has a way of fooling, tricking, beating and dismissing you, still you must never ever give up! When it seems as if your hopes and dreams are lost and others continuously disappoint you, keep pushing. You will never lose if you keep trying. Your journey is only over when you have given up. Others will have a final say only when you quit. You will never fail as long as you keep trying. Once you stop you have no chance, you can no longer improve; yet, if you keep fighting for what you believe in, you become more complete with each effort. Every bit of resistance will help build character along the way.

I promise to teach and uplift you. I promise to be your friend; but more importantly, I will be your parent at all times. I will share everything with you and take nothing. Every chance I get I will remember to tell you how much you mean to me. You are the best of me and so much more. I can't wait to look into your eyes and hold you in my arms. You have already made me a better man, and I still yearn to improve for you. You will never be a burden but you will always be a blessing. Thank you for your love. Thank you for your affection. I Love You! I love you! I love you!

## FAMILY

What is the meaning of family? What families are you a part of? Do you believe in a spiritual family? What is your relationship with your immediate family? Do you know of your extended family or the roots from which you came? Do you understand your family's history and how you came to be? Do you believe your family is a good family? Do you love your family?

Some of us are blessed with fantastic families with great love and teachings. Many of us have good families that struggle to maintain a righteous identity. Others have been born into horrid situations where goodness is destroyed by unimaginable terrors. What does your family mean to you? Do you appreciate their sacrifice for you? Have you ever taken time to understand why your family members act the way they do? Is your family productive or destructive? What does your family expect out of you? Do you ever wish you were raised by a different set of people? I've had to ask myself these questions from time to time.

I have had real trouble with trying to understand and grow with my family. There was a time when I was so proud to be a member of my family. I felt unity and strength within our core. I wanted to impress and feel love from my family. Other times I felt I disappointed family members, and then there were times when I became disappointed in their actions and attitude. There were times when I could not believe some of the deception and selfishness that went on. It is very complicated for some of us to determine what we might owe to those who helped raise us and when it might be time to separate from a negative environment.

Please don't mistake, me for some spoiled brat who is not grateful for many lessons and teachings that came about through my family's efforts. I definitely learned to respect my elders. I learned the value of hard work and how to be thrifty. I gained a spiritual faith and learned the importance of service. I learned the importance of common sense, how to help those in need, how to be tidy, and how to want to be better. I learned how to provide for myself and others at a young age. I learned a lot about responsibility.

I also became aware of greed and denial. I witnessed deception and corruption. I saw the power of ego and the stubbornness of pride. Denial became routine and self-worth was at a premium for many. I came to understand how kind acts had hidden agendas behind them. I witnessed bad intentions and foolery masked by insincere smiles and deceiving counsel. I saw judgments passed harshly by those whose past carried much heavier burdens and mistakes.

It can be very hard to pass judgment or critique the ones you love. No matter what transgressions or wrongs that might have been done to you, there is a sense of loyalty and commitment to your blood. Many of the people who might have let you down might have been your heroes or people you looked up to at some time or another. How do you feel when your heroes fall? Do you feel anger, disappointment, pity, or compassion? I think for me the history and past actions of others and their intentions while performing bad actions or mistakes goes a long way with how our relationship may continue and possibly prosper.

Many times in my life I was told to listen and or obey because someone was older or because they were in a position of authority. Never was I told to question those that lead, especially when the leadership in doubt was suffering from bad judgment. I understand that if you live under someone's roof that you should have respect and follow orders until the day when you can find and make your own way. As adolescents we cannot be demanding of those that support and raise us, especially if we benefit from their supervision. It is definitely not easy to shape and influence a young mind while providing that child with the opportunities to succeed. But what happens when the ones leading are just using the youth for their benefit and have no intentions of helping the children reach a level of success?

How do parents work, live in free housing, receive a large amount of child support, and never put one single penny in a savings account for their child's future? How does a married mother set an example of dishonesty and disloyalty? How do parents steal from their children? How do family members do things for children with the expectation that they will owe them for the rest of their lives? Why do family members punish children for their own failures? I never understood how child abusers lose such control at home yet in the real world display such restraint and self-control. How do parents leave their kids to be raised by others and never put forth any effort to be a part of their own flesh and blood's lives? How can some be so selfish and use innocent children like servants with no regard for their futures or well-being? Time and time again I've seen how adults use children to do their bidding and sacrifice a child's aspirations in order to provide the elder ones with comfort and help ease their struggles. Obviously there are worse actions and unimaginable things done to and expected from children all over this world. I mentioned just a few that I have witnessed or experienced firsthand just to be able to relate and describe to many who might also seek perspective on the matter.

It might sound cliché, but I never truly understood love and sacrifice until I had my firstborn child. From the early stages of the first pregnancy, I knew that my personal wants and desires were no longer at the forefront of my responsibilities. Life was no longer about me and everything became about my child. I could better understand and perhaps judge the way adults provide for others and what should be expected of them. As a burning desire of love and service grew from within, I started noticing the lack of effort, selflessness, and sacrifice that was present in my own development. When I knew that I would have a child here on this earth, I understood that my every purpose was to help this being achieve its greatest potential and do everything in my power to establish a road to success.

I found that love has nothing to do with what you are expecting to get; however, it has everything to do with what you are expected to give which should be everything. Sacrifice and service are two of the truest examples of love. No family can survive without love. It is up to any individual to determine whether or not there is enough love and kindness being shared or if their situation is extracting all of their own love from within. Is it in your best interest to find a better way far from those corrupting your goodness? Life is hard and simply running away isn't always the best solution. Sometimes you might have to stand up against those who you may feel a sense of loyalty too. Other decisions may call for you to remain and become the foundation for change. You may have to take on the role of being a leader and set examples for those who might follow your actions.

"I mean to me, I know what good morals are. It would seem you're supposed to disregard good morals when you're living in a crazy bad world. If you're living cursed, how can you live like an angel? If you're in hell, how can you live like an angel? You're surrounded by devils and you're supposed to live like an angel. That's like suicide, You know what I'm sayin'?-Tupac Shakur

At a certain point, I knew I had to take a stand and make a change. I was surrounded by so many who might, deep down inside, have better intentions, but their actions where restricting my progress. I did not disregard my good morals. I tried to enhance them by eliminating the negativity. I took my destiny into my own hands and did not live through the purpose of others. I became focused on the younger generation and how I could be a better example and tool for their progress.

It is not easy to provoke change and stand for what you believe in; if it was, we would all be living in prosperity with no worries or troubles. There are always conflicting beliefs and points of view when it comes to family and friends. That is where our truth and character come into play. No one can deny your beliefs and actions when you have a true purpose and act with love and understanding in your heart. I do not wish harm upon those who oppose growth. I look upon them with mercy as I hope others do so with me. None of us are perfect, I just can't let other's imperfections eliminate my chances for improvement no matter how much I might love them.

I apologize to those who might feel as if I am encouraging others to disobey their families and revolt at all cost for the sake of change. That is far from my intention. My intention is to share my thoughts with the many out there I know are struggling with the same dilemma and conflicting emotions. I also hope to enlighten others who might be so stubborn and stuck in their ways that they might need an outside voice to help them realize that there might be a better way to show our love and commitment to one another. If we put love for each other in everything we do, then positivity will find a way. Put yourself in each other's shoes; promote kindness and understanding in your thoughts and actions. Do more for each other than we do for ourselves. Love and help one another as we pray to have done upon ourselves. That is how I hope to raise my family. True love conquers all. It provokes selflessness, forgiveness, mercy, service, and compassion. It's good to be loved and even better to give it away. Just be sure to protect your levels of love and how and who you share it with. Choose to be around those that will help it nourish and prosper and not take it all away.

# Family isn't always blood. It's the people

# in your life who want you in theirs;

# the ones who accept you for who you are.

# The ones who would do anything

# to see you smile & who

# love you no matter what.

# -Unknown

## LIGHT UP THE DARKNESS- My letter to my role model

Dear Uncle,

Some say that heroes are born. Others would say that heroic values can be instilled in ones persona and through hard work and extreme effort one may display the courage and bravery worthy of being called a hero. I truly believe we have hero qualities and abilities in all of us. It is true many have prepared and forged themselves into the situations that reveal their valiance or nobility. Think of the many heroes you might have and consider their circumstances. I believe we all have situations that present the opportunities for us to be noble in our own right. Whether it's a last second jump shot or a selfless act. Whether it's saving someone's life or raising one. It can be writing the perfect song, or writing the perfect letter. It can be overcoming poverty, or overcoming an illness or disability. I truly believe that through whatever challenge life may hand us, we always have a choice. We have a choice to be bold, a choice to fight, and a choice to do what is right. Most importantly, we have a choice to believe.

It saddens me to hear of your illness and struggles. At times I hear defeat in your voice. Uncle, I want you to know I love you so very much and you are definitely a hero to me. I have not had many authority figures that have loved and forgiven me the way you have. I know that throughout all my troubles, even you probably doubted if I would ever achieve anything good or of substance. However, no matter what, throughout all my faults you continued to love with patience and understanding. Uncle, I want you to know that I believe in you and know that you can will your way to beat this. Please believe in yourself the same way you have believed in so many others. No matter what pains or obstacles others have had you endure, you always believed in their good. I know you have faith, but don't let that faith diminish. Stay the strong man that you are and let your faith, fight and commitment to overcome determine how this thing plays out. I know we can't change our burdens, but we can change our attitudes toward them.

I'm at a real peace right now. I believe in what I'm trying to do and have found what I believe to have meaning and purpose. Please believe that you are a major influence on many of the things that are positive in my actions. I love you guys so much, and I believe that we will overcome. You guys are always in our prayers, and I know that there is a plan for us if we continue to improve ourselves through love and kindness. I appreciate everything you do. Don't stop believing in your strength, physically, mentally, and spiritually.

## FRIENDSHIP

### Portrait of a Friend

I can't give you solutions to all of life's problems, doubts, or fears. But I can listen to you and together we will search for answers.

I can't change your past with all it's heartache and pain, nor the future with its untold stories. But I can be there now when you need me to care.

I can't keep your feet from stumbling. I can only offer my hand that you may grasp it and not fall.

Your joys, triumphs, successes, and happiness are not mine; Yet I can share in your laughter.

Your descisions in life are not mine to make, nor to judge; I can only support you, encourage you, and help you when you ask.

I can't prevent you from falling away from friendship, from your values, from me. I can only pray for you, talk to you and wait fot you.

I can't give you boundaries wich I have determined for you, But I can give you the room to change, room to grow, room to be yourself.

I can't keep your heart from breaking and hurting, but I can cry with you and help you pick up the pieces and put them back in place.

I can't tell you who you are. I can only love you and be your friend.

-Unknown

I grew up not trusting people so I tried to not have friends. I would call most people that I associated with acquaintances. A few individuals and I shared a certain bond of loyalty and respect. We became a close unit and eventually became good friends. Throughout our future endeavors we would come across so many people that we would bring around and in our circle. Out of respect for one another we were at times forced to get along with others that might not have shared the same views or ideas as the rest of us. Our ideas and values of friendship were becoming more forgiving and lenient. I used to be so harsh and unforgiving when it came to friendship and loyalty. To me it was all in or not at all. My enemies' were their enemies. My beliefs and theirs were pretty much the same. We fought the same fights and always had each other's backs.

Well, as I grew and gained perspective, I realized that there are levels of friendship. I could still have or build relationships with people who might not necessarily have an ultimate loyalty to our companionship. I've grown to understand that no matter how good people are, none of us are perfect. So why would I expect perfection from my friends? There were too many times when I held unwarranted grudges against those who I felt were disloyal. I would find myself taking things so personally and focusing on what they weren't doing instead of appreciating what they have done for our friendship. I was more of a taker than a giver. I found myself taking advantage of other's loyalties and pretty much using people. Greed and power can deceive you into justifying your shortcomings and overpower your ability to see with reason.

With closer examination, I found that in many of my relationships I expected everything and sacrificed little. As much as I thought I gave, I was usually selfish when it came to the important decisions. I mean if a friend was ever in danger or in need, I was there. The problem that I recognized was that if we were both in need, I would almost always choose myself first. For most of my relationships I felt that they were not necessities, they were more of a convenience. I felt like I did not need the help or companionship of others. I felt that whatever I wanted to do I could accomplish on my own without anyone's assistance.

At times I am proud of my independence, but still I must not lose sight or appreciation for the service and kindness of others. Many times in life we accomplish our goals and seem to forget the care and assistance that we benefitted from along the way. As I continue to grow and learn, I try to be a better friend and person. I apologize to any friend who I might have misled or let down. I am sorry for my selfishness and pride. I continue to learn each day from the examples of others what it means to be a better friend. Like anyone, I don't want to be taken advantage of or deceived; so I give cautiously but with no prejudice or expectations. I want to be there for others out of appreciation for all the good things that have been done for me. So many times we forget the kind gestures, helping hands, or lucky breaks. I just feel it is my time and a duty that I feel from within to be a great friend. Wanting to be a great friend is a quick decision. Earning the respect and loyalty that comes from great friendships is an ongoing action that becomes stronger with time. My friends may not be perfect, but they are the perfect friends for me. I appreciate all of our trials and tribulations, our triumphs and accomplishments. I am grateful for our relationships and our ability to grow together.

# "No love, no friendship can cross the path of our destiny without leaving some mark on it forever."
# -Francois Muriac

<u>Gratitude</u>

**"Gratitude unlocks the fullness of life. It turns what we have into enough, and more. It turns denial into acceptance, chaos to order, confusion to clarity. It can turn a meal into a feast, a house into a home, a stranger into a friend. Gratitude makes sense of our past, brings peace for today, and creates a vision for tomorrow."**
**-Melody Beattie**

## <u>Journal:-Gratitude</u>

*So I am watching Extreme Makeover and I am truly so happy for this family and so appreciative of everybody's hard work, sacrifice, and sincere hearts going toward helping others. Now, for the first time in a long time, I find my thoughts and emotions being so caring and pure. I believe in the past I might have been a little hesitant in believing such a story of need and giving. Other times in my life I may have felt my story might be more deserving; however, as I watch this disabled child and his family crippled by life's adversities, I truly felt so very blessed. Blessed with a strong physical and able body. Blessed with the ability to obtain and process knowledge. Blessed with emotions that help me feel what I believe to be right and wrong. Blessed with an inner desire that I can always feel pushing from within, reminding me not to ever settle and always strive to be my very best.*

## <u>Journal:-Gratitude-Simple things</u>

*I sit and think how grateful I am to be alive. I am so appreciative of each day and the opportunity I have to improve myself and become a better person. I am grateful to be able to experience so many wonderful things this world has to offer. We so easily take for granted such luxuries as being able to read a good book, watch an awesome sporting event, and admire anything beautiful and to our liking. Imagine not being able to see the smiling faces of those you love so dearly. Now imagine not being able to hear the roar of an engine, the chorus of your favorite song, the thunder of a vibrant crowd, even the quiet little sounds nature has to offer. Contemplate not being able to hear the most influential and/or inspiring conversations you might have had in your life today. Imagine not being able to taste or feel. Think about being sick your entire life. Imagine not having the ability to think or comprehend. Or maybe you have the ability to think immensely; however, you might not have the ability to express yourself in any way, shape, or form. Our world is filled with the ungratefully blessed. Before you cry or complain, count your blessings.*

**"Let us rise up and be thankful, for if we didn't learn a lot today, at least we learned a little, and if we didn't learn a little, at least we didn't get sick, and if we got sick, at least we didn't die; so, let us all be thankful."**
**-Buddha**

I am so very grateful for the kindness of others. I am so appreciative of so many who have endured such terrible circumstances before me. Thank you for pushing forward and continuing to exist. Thank you to the innocent children who prove to me each day that love truly does still reside and can inspire in the darkest of places. Thank you to all the people of service who continue with selfless acts to help so many in need. I thank you for your example. I am grateful for any and every piece of art or music that has relayed stories of struggle and encouragement, I thank you for your voice. I am appreciative of the many stories in forms of entertainment that relieve my stress and inspire myself to do more. I thank those friends and family that have pure hearts and are always there if needed. I am grateful for all my adversities and people who oppose my progress. I am grateful to those with such anger, hate, and jealously and how your resistance strengthens me. I am grateful for the bad examples that help me understand why I should choose to do good actions. I am grateful every day for a chance to experience and learn from both my mistakes and accomplishments. I am grateful for the chance to evolve and build, not only for myself but for the next generation. I see value in all things and accept the challenge of overcoming wrong in order to appreciate right. I appreciate the journey and opportunities that lie ahead.

**"May we never let the things we can't have, or don't have, or shouldn't have, spoil our enjoyment of the things we do have and can have. As we value our happiness let us not forget it, for one of the greatest lessons in life is learning to be happy without the things we cannot or should not have."**
**-Richard L. Evans**

## THE FRIENDLY GHOST

The accident was unfortunate and it was a difficult time when I first passed. Most of my family and friends shared a common spiritual faith. Still, with all the sadness and mourning, I just wanted to comfort them and let it be known that everything was okay. It's crazy how things can seem so simple and expected when you have true knowledge and experience from another perspective. I think about how I used to be so fearful of death, lost time, and wasted opportunities. Like most of us, I had more of a hope than a true belief of life beyond the one I was living. Yet, now as I watch the ones I love struggle with the reality of my untimely death, I seem to forget how, until now, I too lacked the knowledge or faith to truly understand that things were going to be just fine.

It is great up here, a lot like down there. For the most part everyone is happy. Still, there is some sort of division among certain groups of people. Some never get to experience the pleasure of this paradise; they remain in some lost space. Others seem to be settled in a harsher environment. Even for those that make the joyous trip to this utopia, there is a certain unsettlement and sense of regret among some individuals.

Certain souls walk around with great pride. They gaze upon the living and relate to the many different lives that are overcoming adversity as they push their talents and abilities to the greatest of heights settling for nothing but their very best. There is a great history kept here. Our lives on earth are our movies that are played before all that reside here before we enter the beautiful gates. Everything from our deepest weaknesses and tragic failures to our most outstanding accomplishments and loving actions are revealed to all. No deception or lies just truth, honesty, and pure character is revealed.

How great is your story that will be revealed to the masses? Will you be embarrassed, ashamed, or disappointed in your life's story or will you be grateful for the opportunity and satisfied with your effort and evolution? How did you handle adversity? Did you accomplish your goals? Did you do more for others than you did for yourself? Did you learn from your mistakes and try to become better with each opportunity that came your way?

Some souls stay in that lost space because they feel incomplete and are unable to present their product out of fear and shame. They believe their stories to be unfinished or they are displeased with their final products. They are searching for a way to rewrite their stories. It has been said that some mercy has been granted from time to time to restless souls after many years of torment waiting to get that chance again. Some say that when they are given that chance, most are unaware of their previous existence and once again find themselves falling to the same obstacles and weakness that defeated them before. I guess the point is, if you don't take the time and make the effort to do it right the first go around, what guarantees do you have that you will do better with another opportunity?

Knowing what I know now I periodically leave the comforting gates to dwell among the ones they like to call ghosts. Most are lost and full of regret and dwell on their lives as they watch the living and ponder about what might have been. I, however, am one of those that hang around for different types of reasons. Yes, I miss my family and loved ones tremendously, but I have a true knowledge now that we will be together again at some point. The reason I stay involved with the physical life is to help provide aid and support in any way to those I cherish so dearly. I do subtle things like leave the television on certain inspiring channels and put bookmarks on certain pages that reveal knowledge or inspiration. I bring a comforting presence in times of need and help find misplaced keys and remotes. Obviously there are limits to my capabilities and boundaries that cannot be crossed, but I do my best despite my limitations to provide support.

It's overwhelming at times watching the ones you love and their everyday struggles. To see everyone's imperfections and also honorable actions through everyday circumstances is astounding at times. It's interesting to see how much we react to emotions and how greatly they affect our decisions. So many times I just want to grab the ones I love and tell them not to be so mad, that things should not bother them so much, or that the sadness is just temporary and things get so much better if they are willing to let them. More than anything I want them to understand that they are writing their story and how great it can be if they continue to work extremely hard and believe in themselves. If they only had a true knowledge and understanding of how they already have the lead role and possess all the talents, tools, and abilities needed to create a wonderful tale of great achievement and love. I don't want them to be among those that fall short of greatness from simple negligence, lack of effort, and little perseverance. There are so many options and alternative endings of greatness, and I want to help them understand those opportunities so that we may enjoy our time together beyond the gates and share great stories with each other with no regrets or sadness. I want us to know that we never settled for anything less than our very best and always did everything possible to help others along the way.

## Conclusion

No matter what I think I've done, it is not enough. No matter how many hardships or obstacles that may have been put in my path, they are limited compared to the many miracles and blessings that have influenced and enhanced my quality of life. I am grateful for every breath, every step, every joy, and every pain. I am thankful for the ability and opportunity to live. There is no greater miracle in life than the chance to live one.

I apologize for my shortcomings. At times I am ashamed by my selfish acts and thoughts. Still, I don't regret my situation or my actions. I have lived and grown throughout all my experiences. I do, however, regret not taking action many times in my life. I regret not believing in myself more. We all have confidence, but do we have the true belief in our abilities to stay disciplined and pursue our dreams endlessly? I regret not helping others as much as I should. I regret not being ready for opportunities that could have changed my life and those dearest to me because of my lack of preparation and focus. I regret not having the knowledge necessary to properly defend my rights and the rights of those that I love dearly. I regret not putting in the effort necessary to fulfill my potential.

I somehow realized that I was no more special than anyone else. We all can be great if we choose to be. No one is better than the other when we are at our best. Previously, I fooled myself into thinking that God owed me some special blessings. I thought because my heart was good and that I mostly intended to do what was right that I deserved some good fortune. I thought that because I have experienced so much tragedy and pain that I somehow would be given success and happiness. I would tell myself time and time again that if I didn't receive a certain amount of prosperity, then I would give up and follow a path less positive and restrictive. It took a lot of wrong choices and bad mistakes to help me understand that there is no perfect path; however, the alternative to choosing to do right is nothing but ultimate suffering.

Every time you ever want to give up, think of the alternative. Are you going to quit? Are you going to fold under pressure? When we feel pain, is it better to also inflict suffering on others or to help bring joy to those in need? Are we angry at our shortcomings or happy for the opportunity to make things right? Each and every one of us is unique in our own right. The greatness inside us is stronger than any obstacles that may stand in our way. Every day is a chance to become the person we always were meant to be.

It's okay if you're not okay as long as you haven't given up! It's okay if your confused, lost, or abused, alone and scared, or stuck in a slump. The most important thing is to never, ever give up! Billions of dollars are spent every day trying to tell us what can make us happy, what we should look like, what our limitations are, and what we should or should not be. There is death and life, and there is no life if you are not fighting for something. Do not find yourself in the waiting place waiting for good fortune to come your way. Fight! Fight for what you believe in; fight for your identity and success. Fight to be somebody in this world. Fight to do what is right. Fight to find what is right for you!

**Strong Inside:- A Relentless Pursuit of Continuous Improvement.** Each and every one of us has been blessed with inner strength. No matter who you are, where you're at, or what you've been through, know that you are strong enough to be whatever it is your heart desires. Don't make excuses, make a difference. Be true to yourself, help others, and make each day your masterpiece. The world can be a dark place. Light up that darkness with your relentless pursuit of happiness. We all have a responsibility to ourselves to live the wonderful life we are capable of. It is our greatest gift and greatest responsibility. Every day we are blessed with a chance to learn and become stronger. Every day we are blessed with the opportunity to become better people. Don't let your fears prevent you from achieving your goals.

I am grateful for the opportunity to share my thoughts and feelings with you. Hopefully I have touched you with a bit of positivity, compassion, and understanding. I hope that I may have inspired or just reminded others that we all have a special place in this world. It is up to us to remain dedicated and disciplined to fulfill our potential. Let's come together to make this world a better place, each and every day, one step at a time.